The Greatest Guide to
Relationships and Dating

This is a **GREATEST**GUIDES title

Greatest Guides Limited, Woodstock, Bridge End, Warwick CV34 6PD, United Kingdom

www.greatestguides.com

Series created by Harshad Kotecha

Greatest Guides is committed to a sustainable future for our planet. This book is printed on paper certified by the Forest Stewardship Council.

MIX
Paper
FSC FSC® C020837

Printed and bound in the United Kingdom

ISBN 978-1-907906-05-3

This book is dedicated to anyone out there who has ever felt either the joy or the pain that love can bring – hopefully it will bring you more of the former and less of the latter.

Contents

A few words from Jenni …

'Love makes the world go round' or so says the song. From the moment we can walk and talk, we are introduced to the concept of Love with a capital 'L'. No sooner has it been established that 'Mummy and Daddy love you' then you are catapulted into the world of fairytales and nursery rhymes. From Adam and Eve, to Cinderella and Prince Charming; Mickey and Minnie, to Shrek and Fiona. Love stories surround us on billboards, tv ads, magazines – there is nowhere we can turn to avoid being bombarded with the idea that 'Love is all you need'.

Before we start on our journey through the ins-and-outs of Love, I'd like you to define for yourself exactly what you think Love is; and exactly what you think Love isn't. Clarifying your thoughts at the beginning will be invaluable. It will do a lot towards helping you understand your past behaviors. It will help show you what you've done 'right' in the past. It will probably also show you where and how you might have gone off the track. This is crucial information, so we don't keep making the same 'mistakes' over and over, which is what most of us do.

What I am hoping to accomplish with this book is to give you a 'wise auntie' at your fingertips. Practical, no-nonsense advice on all the different aspects of meeting people, starting relationships and nurturing them. Sometimes, with the best will in the world, it might go wrong so I will also share with you some advice on how to extricate yourself from an unhappy relationship. We will also talk about dealing with the pain. Starting over. Finding strength to do that and how to begin the process. How to believe in yourself again. All the things you need to know to get back up on that horse.

Hopefully, in this small book, you will find a lifetime of answers.

Good luck!

Jenni

"One word frees us of all the weight and pain of life. That word is love." Sophocles

Love in the 21ˢᵗ Century

66 He has achieved
success who has lived well,
laughed often, and loved
much. **99**

Bessie Stanley

Chapter 1
Love in the 21st Century

When I was a little girl, there was a wonderful schoolyard poem:

"Jenni and Colin sitting in a tree,
K-I-S-S-I-N-G,
First comes love,
Then comes marriage
Then comes Jenni pushing the baby carriage."

Wasn't it wonderful when life was that simple? You knew exactly what was expected of you, exactly where you were going, and just what you would find when you got there. There was a blueprint of what life was meant to be like and a map to show you the way. There were specific ages at which you did things and certain ways in which they were done. There wasn't much straying from The Rules and, if you did, it was only something mildly adventurous, like getting married on an island in the Caribbean or maybe living together for a few months before the big day.

Welcome to the 21st Century – now *anything* goes – or just about. Things that our parents or grandparents would *never* have been able to come up with in their wildest dreams, or worst nightmares, are now a matter of course and no one bats an eyelid.

What does this mean to us? Well, to be successful at anything in life, it is really important to have a clear understanding of whatever the concept is that you're about to approach. Relationships are no different. It isn't that there is only one way to look at relationships – but it's *crucial* to know how *you* perceive them.

When you hear Men, Women, Relationships, Children, and Sex – what images spring to mind? What definitions do *you* have for these words?

What is *your* definition of 'The Perfect Relationship'? What does it look like? What does it feel like? How will you know when you have it? The reason we're going through all of this now is because, like anything else in life, *you'll first need to know where you want to end up before you can figure out how best to get there…*

There is a very common problem that most of us (myself included) have – and I've not heard anyone else discussing it in magazines or books, so pay close attention… it's a bit tricky to grasp at first but, if you were clever enough to buy this book, then you're clever enough to get it ☺ are you ready?…

One of the biggest causes of difficulties with having a successful working relationship nowadays is that most of us are living 21st Century lives yet still using 20th Century rules.

What that means is that we're still thinking of ourselves and relationships through what we learned in the last century. Our references could have been anything from a Hollywood movie to Shakespeare. Frank Sinatra to Nellie Furtado. Soap operas on the telly or the 'How To Get A Man' articles in your favorite magazine. Whatever they are, these last century references just don't work anymore. Think of trying to stick a CD into an iPad; old fashioned technology in a new-fashioned world.

If you want to make your love life work today, you'd best be certain that you're up to speed with the way things are now. Yes, of course, Love – with a capital L – is still pretty much the same but the components and the journey are quite different indeed.

Let's run through some basics and see what your current perceptions are… you might feel that none of this applies to you, in which case, just feel free to jump ahead and get stuck in to the rest of the book…

THEN versus NOW...

MEN:

Last Century...

Men were the providers. They headed up the family and went out to earn the money needed to run the household. They made most of the major decisions – at least we let them think they did. The Man of the House chose the car, chose the house, the holidays and what the family watched on the television. He paid for it all, so there was an unwritten belief that as he owned the kingdom it was his to rule as he saw fit. No matter how amenable his personality, there wasn't a lot of disagreement that went on. If you wanted to change his mind about something, and you were the wife, you used trickery. If you were the child, you asked your mother to plead your case and she used trickery on your behalf. Outside of the home, society pretty much encouraged this 'king of all he surveys' concept so men were catered to in all situations. From the office to the pub, from the church to the football stadium, dining table to living room sofa – there was never a question of 'Who's the Daddy?' – you always knew it was the big hairy fella in the trousers. A pretty good gig was this being The Man thing, definitely nice work if you had the necessary equipment to get it.

This Century...

The ball certainly does bounce differently these days! ☺ There's a good chance that the 21st Century man might not be the main provider. You'll also be hard put to find a household where the man of the house is still 'in charge'. He certainly isn't ruling any kingdom and he'll be lucky if he is choosing anything more important than 'spinach or broccoli?' But don't play the violins for him just yet because, on the upside, the lessening of his position has freed him up to now be who he might *really* want to be. 21st Century man's choices are more relaxed. He doesn't have to marry and have a family if he doesn't wish to. He gets asked out on dates a lot more than before and he won't always be expected to pay. His life is easier now if he is gay – in most sections of society it is accepted and isn't necessarily considered 'un-manly' in the way it might have been say 20 years ago. There is more of a chance for him to pursue the career that he desires, rather than whatever job will give him the money to support the family even if he hates it. He might be less stressed out these days, as he has an equal partner to share the burdens with. And he might be happier because his 'other half' really is his equal and not a subordinate employee. He most likely has a better relationship with his children and he now experiences the previously unknown joys of changing nappies and attempting to calm down toddler tantrums in the supermarket. He is acquainted with the vacuum cleaner and the ironing board – though sometimes he has to be pointed in their direction – and it isn't unheard of for him to be the better cook of the partnership.

What this means in the scheme of things… It means that men are a lot more fun to be around (if you're a woman). And, if you're a man, it means that life is a lot less scary. Yes, some men will tell you that they're now 'confused', they don't know if they should bring flowers or hold the door open. They don't know what's expected of them anymore and they feel they're always getting it wrong. But I think older ones are enjoying having more choice as to who they want to be and the younger ones now have the incredible freedom of making it up as they go along. You might be a househusband taking charge of the home and the children; you might be the one who took 'leave' when the baby was born. You might be the one who runs the house – now it's up to the two people involved about what exactly the role of the man is going to be.

WOMEN:

Last Century…

If you were a woman towards the end of the last century, much of the time from your mid-teens to early 20's was devoted to Catching a Man. If you were lucky enough, you 'got' one when you were 15 or 16 and held on for dear life until you waltzed down the aisle on his arm. In those days, in the words of Beyonce, *'If you want it you'd better put a ring on it'*, so of course Simon obligingly took your hand and put a ring on it. Then you could breathe. You were married and your name went from being 'Poor Helen Who Might Never Get Married' to 'Somebody-or-the-Other's Little Woman'. No one might have called you that to your face, but it was understood that you were definitely Number 2 in this marriage malarkey. Your job was to look nice, behave yourself and be the Perfect Wife. What exactly that meant would, of course, be determined by your husband. You would be told what time to have food on the table in the evening. You would have spent your days tidying the house, taking care of the laundry, taking care of the children, the garden (if there was one); and ironing the socks and underpants if there wasn't. It wasn't ideal but at least you had a man and in Ye Golden Olden Days that was all that really mattered.

This Century…

The lioness has roared and, as the saying goes, 'How are you going to keep her down on the farm once she's seen the big lights of the city?' No longer are we considered The Weaker Sex in or out of the bedroom or the boardroom.

What this means in the scheme of things… If you fall in line with the statistics, you probably have a job or career of your own choosing. You possibly make more money than your partner and, in the workplace, you could quite likely be his boss. You may or may not be married and, other than your mother's persistent whining about it, there's no stigma attached to being single in the 21st Century. You will get married if and when you feel like it. You are your own woman and aren't in any big hurry to become 'Vernon's missus' or 'Clarabelle's mummy'. Yes, you probably do want to meet someone; we all know it's great to have something to warm your feet against on a cold winter's night. But do you believe you can have a good life without that happening? You probably do. If and when you do meet someone, you will have an equal voice in setting up your life in a way that works for you. If you have children, you won't be expected to give up your career. If you decide not to have children, other than your mother nagging, you won't be a social pariah. And if, sadly, it all goes belly-up, statistics show that there's a pretty good chance you'll get another go at having a successful relationship – even with your kids in tow. The down sides are that you're quite likely still carrying most of the load of keeping the house ticking over but you'll see that later on I have a few tips on how to change that so that everyone is pitching in and the burden isn't all on you. The other major downside is that you might suffer from the 'I thought I could have it all' syndrome that so many now have. Well you can't have it *all*. You can have most of it, but not all of it, so choose wisely…

We've covered the two most important components of this relationship business: Us and Them – name your gender and choose your side ☺

Let's now do a quick run-through of some of the other aspects that have changed, so you can roadcheck your attitudes to be sure you're 'getting with the program' as the kids say…

COUPLES:

Last Century…

A couple was a man and a woman. Usually similar in age, socio-economic background, religion and often, quite spookily, they even looked like each other. Usually married – not living together. Usually brought together by friends, family, other villagers or whatever folk exchanged a chicken, a camel and a bag of grain for the privilege.

This Century…

Most of the time it is still one man and one woman and, for the sake of expediency in this book, that will be the configuration we will use. But everything else is up for grabs. She can be 48 while he's 38. He can be very wealthy and met her when she was a waitress at the local Chinese takeaway. She can be Jewish while he's Catholic. If they look like each other, it's probably because they share a hairdresser or plastic surgeon. And as for how they met – well that could be anything from on Facebook to a naturist holiday in Ibiza; a wine-tasting class to a Pilate's retreat.

What this means in the scheme of things... In general, it's a good thing. Your choices are more varied and the opportunities to meet people are greater. You're not as bound by who/where/when/why you can date someone. Families can still be an issue, but, in most areas of society, parents will now at least make an effort to welcome people from different backgrounds into their families. So, yes, the changes are a good thing in general. I do have a few reservations about certain aspects of love and relationships in the 21st Century, but it doesn't matter what I think as there is no way to turn back the clock at this stage. The one thing I would say is that I sometimes worry that we've become spoiled by having so much choice. That maybe we now feel that since the fishing pond is so deep and so full, we can keep casting our line in the hope that the next one that bites will be the big one. Do that for too long and you can find that the sun has gone down and you're off home with no fish.

CHILDREN:

Last Century...

Children were not a debatable question. Unless, sadly, there was a physical reason that made having children impossible, there was no question or doubt but that Helen and Simon were going to have children. And not 'a child' but children. When the children started arriving, Helen – if she had a job of some description – left it. Quite often, she would go from having one child to another so it could sometimes be 10 – 15 years before she was free to pickup the reins of her career again; which, of course, by that time had most likely passed her by. What were these children like? They were well behaved, obedient, if they were boys they often had their mothers wrapped around the proverbial little finger. If they were girls they tended to have that special relationship with their fathers. They played happily and safely in the streets with the other neighborhood children (or so we are lead to believe). Their role in the house and in their parent's relationship had moved on from 'children should be seen and not heard' but they had not yet gained the voice that they now have.

This Century...

Many couples no longer choose to have children. Or, if they do, it is quite common for them to wait until at least one of the parents is firmly established in a career. Many couples decide to have one or maybe two children, often with the thought that they will be able to provide better emotionally and financially to a smaller family. Many issues, such as childcare, both parents working, extended families not living in a close radius, schools sometimes being on the other end of town, means that having children brings more pressures to bear than it might have a few decades ago. Also, the separation and divorce statistics being what they are means that many children need to function in divided households, and how we deal with this is one of the biggest difficulties we have had to face in the 21st Century.

What this means in the scheme of things... As a mother of one of these 21st Century rugrats myself, I am well-qualified to comment on the permutations of this 'creature' ☺ Yes, I know they're not all like my son but there are certain things that most of them seem to have in common. 21st Century child tends to be more independent – in thought and deed. They are usually more vocal in their participation in family life than in the past. This can make decision-making in a home more cumbersome but, in the long run, often makes for the better running of a household. Children are also now more likely to be participating in the maintenance of the house, vacuuming, laundry, cooking simple meals – my son has been doing all those since he was 14, and so do many of his friends. This makes certain aspects of home life easier and, if handled correctly, definitely cuts down on the burden that used to fall completely on the shoulders of the woman of the house. The divided households issue, however, still needs to be dealt with. Statistics tell us that it is going to happen, but, in the 21st Century, too many of us really don't know how to handle ending relationships without damaging what is usually the most precious product of the relationship. Just because the relationship broke down doesn't mean that all the pieces need to be smashed to bits as well. Beware of the emotional safety of your children… but there is more on that in the following chapters.

SEX:

Last Century…

It depends on how far back in the century you're going. If you're going way back, then the role of the man was to do it when he felt like it, how he felt like it, and sometimes with whom he felt like doing it with. The job of the woman in those days was to lie back and think of her favorite movie star until it was time to 'fake it'. Later on in the last century, things got slightly better in some ways, but decidedly worse in others. Yes it became acceptable for women to want sex, have sex and even initiate sex. But, along with all that, came the obligations of looking better than anyone else, being better at it than anyone else – all in the name of holding on to 'Your Man', or, in some cases, getting someone else's. And if you didn't have the best lingerie, know the best moves, and be ready, willing and more able than most, then there would be a good chance that his attention would be grabbed by the new girl in Accounting.

This Century…

Maybe it's just in my life ☺ but I do think things have calmed down a bit. I think there is a less frenetic edge to Being the Best. It's ok for men to have a bit of a belly and thinning hair – we don't think they all need to look like George Clooney or that Pattinson fella. And, because there are so many Angelina Jolie look-alikes pouring out of the plastic surgery clinics, I think that men are actually starting to hanker after women who look like 'real' women. Or, once again, maybe that's just in my life ☺

What this means in the scheme of things… It means that the sexual aspect of a relationship is, in the main, a lot easier. We now tend to regard it as a healthy part of our relationship, rather than a necessary obligation. For some of us in certain relationships, sex might be what the entire relationship is about. I don't think that is necessarily an emotionally healthy approach. If you position yourself (no pun intended) in a certain way, be careful that doesn't become the only way in which you are regarded. Being a sex god or goddess can be fun but if that's your only calling card, when someone decides to settle down, they may head off in another direction. No one wants to swing from the chandeliers *all the* time.

THE BOTTOM LINE…

Much is the same in the 21st Century; but much is also different. Take a moment to be sure that you don't still have a fairytale idea of what a perfect relationship is, one that is no longer relevant in today's society. Be sure that you're not waiting for a knight on a white horse, or kissing a lot of frogs in the hope that one of them will turn into a prince. Be sure that you're not kissing a sleeping beauty or looking for someone whose tootsies will fit into your glass slipper. You want to be certain that you're not expecting to have a relationship exactly like your parents or grandparents, because we're now living in a *very* different world. A lot was simpler in Ye Golden Olden Days. It was easier to be romantic, you knew what the rules were and life was easy if you stuck to them. It's all quite complicated now. There's more to know and further to go. We could spend weeks debating which was the better time, but the fact is that, like it or not, we're now in the 21st Century so let's make it work for us and our loved ones… even if we haven't yet met them ☺ Now let's get cracking…

Finding Love

66 Dating is like going on a job interview. You don't know if you'll get the job, but if you do well, you get to see the interviewer naked. **99**

Anonymous

Chapter 2
Finding Love

Many of us spend most of our waking moments, consciously or not, looking for love. Often in the wrong places and usually with methods that are almost guaranteed to sabotage our efforts before we even begin.

Over the years, as a counselor, presenter of television relationship programs, advice columnist, giver of dating seminars, author – and, of course, someone who has herself danced the dance of love – I have picked up more than my fair share of tips on the How, Where, When and Why of meeting people.*** I have watched others and learned from their mistakes, and I have observed myself and learned from my own. I have read the great and the good, and have spoken with the wise and wonderful around the globe. What have I learned? Well, you're about to find out…

How to meet new people

The easiest way is to open yourself up to the possibility. 'There are no good ones out there', 'All the good ones are taken', or any of those phrases you'll hear around the makeup counter at the shopping mall guarantee failure. When I say to people 'You're a good one and you're not taken!' they usually mumble 'Well that's different'. Which, I assume, translates to 'Actually I'm not really a good one but maybe I'll be able to fool someone into thinking I am'. You may not be perfect but that's OK because neither is anyone else. Somewhere out there is someone who has the same proportion of pluses and minuses as you, and think how much fun you can have finding them!

Increasing your options

Keep yourself open to meeting all sorts of new people. The more people you meet, the greater the chance that you'll meet someone you want to have a relationship with. One of the biggest mistakes that we make is to restrict ourselves to the types of new people we want to meet. We only want to meet men, or women, or people of this age or that religion or the other background. Not so. *Meet everyone!* Young, old, married, single, male, female. Just because the person standing in front of you isn't the type of person you currently imagine as your future partner, that doesn't mean that person isn't part of their circle of friends and acquaintances.

Be open, be friendly, and find out what is interesting about each person you meet. Ask them about themselves, tell them about yourself, and, in no time, you'll find that you're meeting lots of new people and making new friends – that's when you'll meet that certain someone.

Where to meet new people

Where is the best place to meet people? On the bus, at a wedding, in the supermarket – I've known people to meet new partners at funerals. *Any time or place that has more than one person present is a possible opportunity to meet someone.* Longer working hours, busier lives, distance from our families, and no longer living in heavily structured communities, have all contributed to some of the difficulties we now face regarding meeting new people. However, some ingenious solutions have come into play, and meeting new people has never been easier, if you're willing to give it a go…

Friends – Meeting people through friends has always been a good method. **Pros:** Chances are, you will already have shared interests and values. You'll often be able to check each other out from a distance before taking the step of spending time together away from the group. **Cons:** You have to be *really* careful with these types of relationships, if it goes wrong you may cause problems within the original group. Meeting through friends is brilliant, when it works, but it can be disastrous when it doesn't – so tread carefully.

Family – I once did a television series based on whether or not your friends and family could pick a better partner for you than you would pick yourself. Guess what? They often can. Your family knows and loves you – warts and all – and they are more likely to be capable of knowing what you *need* rather than what you *want*. Though nothing is more excruciatingly embarrassing than when, on your 30th birthday, your mother (who is even more desperate for you to be part of a couple at this point than you might be) drags someone home from the Sears parking lot that she 'just knew you would love because he looks *just* like that nice teacher from Glee'…

Love at WORK – When I first started working, my grandmother gave me an invaluable bit of advice. 'Don't relieve yourself in the same location in which you eat' – which loosely translates to 'don't go out with people you work with'. Some of you will say 'Where else am I to meet people?', my answer is anywhere else but here. If it goes right, you run the risk of losing the respect of your co-workers, damaging your chances for promotion (especially if you're female) and becoming the focus of everyone's water-cooler chats. Nowadays, many companies will have a clause in your initial employment agreement that makes romantic relationships cause for dismissal, so that takes care of that.

If the relationship ends – which they often do – that is when it can really get unpleasant. My inbox is constantly filled with emails saying 'I was dating this guy in my office, now we've split up and he's telling everyone my private business'. Usually, someone who dates once in an office will make a habit of it. So when your big romance ends chances are you're going to have to sit there and watch him sneaking off behind the copy machine with someone else. Yes, it *is* possible to meet the love of your life anywhere. But *please* try your best to ensure that it is somewhere other than the workplace.

Love on the Internet – The past ten years has seen meeting on the internet overtake just about any other form of hooking-up out there. Initially, most people met through chat rooms (a virtual 'room' where people with a common interest chat in a group) – many still do. Then came dating sites, discussion forums, social networking sites, and all are flourishing. I have attended weddings that sprang from meetings on the internet. Christenings of babies born from people who met on an internet site and decided that maybe touching each other might be more enjoyable than touching a keyboard.

Everyone is doing it, young, old and inbetween – I have even engaged in a spot of internet romance myself. The internet works well in a time when a lot of people are really busy, and some of us, believe it or not, are quite shy. Meeting people on the internet gives you a chance to get to know them at your own pace. For those of us who are single with children, it is brilliant because we get a chance to meet and get to know people without spending a fortune on babysitters. Also great if you live out in the country and dropping into the nearest Starbucks isn't an option.

The best thing about the internet is that it brings you together with like-minded souls. Type in 'I like rodeos' or 'Oreos should be a major food group' and you will instantly access a couple thousand folks within shouting distance who feel the same way. If you're a bit on the shy side, I advise going to sites that are about a shared interest rather than 'here's my picture do you like the look of me?' All the normal rules – such as 'don't give out personal information, don't meet up with strangers in unsafe locations, be honest in your descriptions' – apply.

Love through Personal ads – There is a marvelous book called *Round Heeled Woman,* about a woman in her 60s who ran a personal ad and then spent the following year keeping company with the various gentlemen who responded. For the literary amongst us with a good turn of phrase, personal ads can be the way to go. However, first you have to get past the vernacular: GSOH (Good Sense of Humor), DWK (Divorced With Kids), and FC (Follically Challenged – bald). Then you have to decide where to place the ad. Are you a New York Times reader, Readers Digest, or People Magazine? – Whichever publication you read, chances are they have a personal ads section. You pay to place the ad; they give you a contact location (number, post box, or email address) through which the respondents contact you. You decide which responses are appealing and begin a correspondence. With the advent of the internet, personal ads are not as popular as they used to be, but for the faint-hearted it is easier, as the pace is slower.

Love through Speed dating – Definitely for the brave among us! A group of people meet in a large room where there are individual tables with chairs on either side. A timer is set for, usually, 5 minutes and you have a chance to make whatever impression you can on the person on the other side of the table. The whistle blows and you move on to the next table. And so on and so on. At the end of the evening, a moderator adds up the scores and you find out who would like to possibly get to know you better. Speed dating can be fun if you go in a group, or if you don't take it too seriously. Go to a session where you will be with similar people to yourself. I once observed a session of young investment professionals and it was like sharks at a feeding frenzy. Speed dating originally came out of the Orthodox Jewish community as a way for young people to meet each other while staying within the bounds of propriety – it has certainly moved on a long way since then!

Activities – For my money, this might be the best way to meet people; possibly because it always worked for me. ☺ Think of something you would like to learn, find a place that has a course in it, sign up for the course and you're away. The benefit of this method is that, if you don't meet anyone, you will still walk away with a magnificent piece of pottery or a horse's head that you sculpted yourself. Commonsense is appropriate here. If you are looking for a big hairy outdoorsy guy, then perhaps a lace-making course is not the way to go, nor is 'How to do acrylic nails at home'. If there isn't anything you want to learn, then join a club that does something that you enjoy, like scuba diving or bike riding. It is a lot less pressured when you do something with a group of people who share an interest – you're engaging in an activity you already like doing and if you meet someone, that's an added bonus!

Love through Dating agencies – A comprehensive form profiling your personality and what you're looking for is filled out by you. A fee is exchanged – which can be anything from $50 to $10,000 (and don't assume that the higher the fee the better the service). Then the nice people who work at the dating agency will look though their client list and see who they have on their register who most matches up with your data, and what you are looking for. They will choose a small selection, usually about three or four, they will then send you mini-dossiers on the people and you can choose whether or not. It makes total sense, and it does work for many. However, there are three things you need to watch out for.

The first is that you need to be totally honest when filing out your application, and so do they. Descriptive phrases are sometimes used with reckless abandon by the ladies, so watch out for words like 'slim', 'young', 'blonde'. While the gentlemen sometimes get a bit carried away with phrases referring to their finances, so 'almost millionaire' (yes I have seen that) and 'financially solvent' can often mean just the opposite. Also be aware that, often, if someone is stumping up a lot of money for such a service, it might mean they are overly zealous in their search – if that doesn't pose a problem for you then this method might work.

Last, but probably most important, is the ability of the people running the dating service to appreciate you as an individual, not just matching you up with another set of comparable ticked boxes. I have seen some spectacular successes from dating agencies, so if you're really serious then give it a try, but remember to interview the agency thoroughly before plunking down your hard-earned cash.

" Confidence is the sexiest thing a woman can have. It's much sexier than any body part. "

Aimee Mullins

When to meet new people

Anytime can be the right time to meet people. For some reason, there seems to be an idea that Meeting People is a specific activity. We are going out to 'meet people' is the cry heard as the weekend rolls round. You can meet people *anytime*. However, this conversation is probably more about when *not* to meet people. Many of us look at love as the cure-all for any of life's ills, so, at the first sign of trouble on the horizon, we fling ourselves into finding love. We're bored – it's time to meet someone. We have a real issue that needs dealing with and meeting someone becomes a diversion to keep you away from the real task at hand. Then there are the folk who, immediately upon the ending of a relationship, decide 'Yes, right – let's rush right out and find a replacement'. For the record, that is the absolute *worst* time to go looking for love.

Almost anytime can be a good time to meet people; just do a quick review on yourself. Check that you really are in the right frame of mind for something that, while enjoyable and rewarding, can also be taxing. In other words – don't put on the uniform if you don't really have the energy for the game.

What to keep in mind

Many of us launch ourselves into the dating world with the purposefulness of Napoleon planning a military campaign. There is an air of grim determination that I have seen on the faces of people, accompanied by the dreaded phrase 'I just *have* to meet someone'. The look in their eyes would be guaranteed to scare the life out of anyone who may accidentally come across their path; and the phrase 'deer in headlights' certainly springs to mind. Nothing scares people away more than feeling that they are a trophy to be acquired. People want to come towards you naturally, not be dragged by force. Keep in mind that the law of nature is such that what you search for most diligently is often the most difficult to find. Think of it as looking for fun. Start out with the concept that you are hoping to meet someone with similar interests and outlook as yourself. Then add on 'someone I am attracted to who is attracted to me', 'someone I want to get to know better'. If there is really something there, it will grow naturally. There is nothing that will throw a spanner in the works faster than two people meeting each other, there is a small attraction, and one launches into a mission to trap the other at all costs. If it's real, it will happen.

Asking someone out

In my experience, I have never heard of anything particularly disastrous happening to someone who asked a person out on a date. There are basically two things that can happen: 1) They say 'yes'… or 2) They say 'no'. Most of us tend to totally ignore the possibility of it being a 'yes' and focus totally on *it-will-be-no-and-lightning-will-strike-me-down-and-I-shall-be-humiliated-for-the-rest-of-my-life.* First, let's not forget that you often get what you focus on. Approaching the situation with the hope of a positive outcome is more likely to gain you a positive outcome. Next let's keep in mind that the world will not end if the person says no. It does not mean you are a bad person, an unattractive person, a dislikable person. Neither does it mean that no one will ever like you and you are destined to spend your life on the scrapheap of life. It just means that, at this particular time, this particular person is not inclined. Here are a few pointers to ease the process of asking someone out:

1. Don't think about it for 6 months while you try to get up the courage. *Just do it!*

2. Don't discuss it with all your family, friends, and the postman. *Just do it!*

3. Don't do it in front of other people or in a public place, with all your friends and their friends standing around watching.

4. If possible, maybe you're shy, there is nothing wrong with asking by email or text. By the way, while it is acceptable to ask by these methods, it is never acceptable to cancel by these methods.

5.   Keep it simple and to the point 'I was wondering if you would be interested in going for a cup of coffee some time?'

Before the date

Keep in mind that this is just a date, nothing more – nothing less. For a brief period of time, two people are going to engage in activities they both enjoy. You will attempt to get to know more about each other. This is NOT a-job-interview-to-determine-the-outcome-of-the-rest-of-your-life; so chill out. Don't overthink the date. I am constantly hearing 'I met him/her, I thought we would get along and we went on a date and she was a totally different person. What a nut-job!'

It's difficult, but try not to discuss your upcoming date with the entire world. You may be proud, excited, nervous – but the more people you discuss it with before, the more people you'll have to discuss it with after. Wait until you know if there is anything to talk about before blabbing to all and sundry.

Wear comfortable clothing. Ladies try on your outfits before you go. Walk around the house for half an hour. If you have to hold in your stomach, tug it up, tug it down, can't breathe in it, then for heaven's sake don't wear it. 'She spent the whole night tugging her skirt down, what was that all about?' Comfortable shoes are also a good idea. It might sound to you that I am saying go in your jimjams and slippers – I am not. However, unless you are going for a job interview as a lap dancer, there is no need to present yourself as one. Especially on first dates, when you're not yet certain of what sort of relationship you want to have. Don't advertise something that might not be on offer.

During the date (yes)

One of the secrets to having people like you in any situation is for you to make them feel better about themselves for having spent time with you. How do you do that? Pay attention to them. Ask questions and listen to their answers. Ask more questions based on what they've said (which makes them realize that you've been listening). Find out what they're interested in. What music they like. How they spend their spare time. Where they like to go on holiday.

However, be careful how you do this. Don't make it seem like you're going down a checklist. Avoid questions like 'What sort of car do you drive?' and 'Do you have a savings account?' Stay positive – I know that is difficult for some of us, but give it a whirl. Most importantly – be yourself.

During the date (no)

Don't go on endlessly about yourself. Don't ask questions that sound as if you're a bank officer and they are applying for a mortgage. Do NOT ask questions about their past relationships – there will be time enough for that later. Do NOT volunteer information about your past relationships. Why so many people feel the need to do this I will never understand. Trust me, no good ever comes of it. It creates the impression that you are either bitter or are bringing unnecessary baggage to the table.

After the date (yes)

You've had a good time. You think the other person has had a good time. What happens next? First of all, at the end of the date, be sure to say thank you (even if you've had an awful time – it's only polite). I know it sounds like an accepted fact, but you wouldn't believe how many people don't do it, so don't forget to say 'Thank you'.

If you really like the person and would like to see them again, it is completely acceptable to say so. 'Thank you, I really enjoyed myself, maybe we can do it again sometime'. Make sure to say it like a casual statement rather than 'ask me on another date right now why don't you?' That could make the other person uncomfortable and feeling as if they're being put on the spot. If you are too shy to say it, then feel comfortable to email or text. However you do it – carrier pigeon or skywriting – be sure to let them know you've enjoyed yourself and would be happy to repeat the experience.

" Golf and sex are about the only things you can enjoy without being good at them. **"**

Jimmy Demaret

After the date (no)

First check the entry directly above. As mentioned, it is a big no-no not to give an indication of whether or not the date was a success from your point of view. But the biggest no-no of all is saying that you'll call if you have no intention in the world of doing so. That is really unkind and leaves that person waiting for something that isn't going to happen. Be honest. However, this does NOT mean 'This was the worst night of my life and I wouldn't go out with you again if you were the last person on earth'. A simple 'Thank you for tonight and good luck with your job interview' is polite but carries no promise of further contact you do not intend to carry through.

Another no-no is discussing your thoughts with anyone who may know the person. Comments like 'watching paint dry', or 'what a loser!' have a way of getting back to the person somehow. It might be true, but you wouldn't like it done unto to you, so don't do it unto them.

Falling in love with friends

One of the most common phenomena these days is people falling in love with close friends. It could be someone you went to college with, a roommate, a best friend's brother – you've been going on holiday together, hanging out together, and, all of a sudden, one day you look up and decide 'uh-oh… I think I like him in That Way!' One of the reasons this happens frequently nowadays is that many of us build walls around ourselves to protect against the people we feel we could possibly have a relationship with. We have our defence systems in place against people we don't want to hurt us (potential partners), but are completely open to people we feel safe with (our friends). As this person gets to see the natural-100% you, it is possible to know each other and develop a walls-down-closeness that might feel like something slightly more than 'just friends'.

Think *very carefully* before you make such a move and move very slowly. Allow yourself room to step back if you have to without having made a total mess of the friendship. Try to keep bedroom antics out of the equation (at least until you are absolutely sure) – that's the step that is most difficult to retreat from with a shred of dignity if it doesn't work out. Difficult but not impossible, I've seen friends cross the line then cross back safely. I've also seen people who were friends for years finally realize that the very thing they had been searching the world for was right under their noses all along.

'Wrong' relationships

We've all had at least one inappropriate relationship – some more 'wrong' than others. The 17-year-old boy at the neighborhood dry cleaners, your ex's sister, your boss, the security guard at the office. My advice, from my advanced years, is to resist the temptation and don't do it. But if you're young and invincible you're not going to want to listen; and if you're not so young and have made a lifetime habit of this then you're not going to want to listen either. So if you have convinced yourself that despite obvious indications to the contrary, this person is The One, just do us both a small favor and ask yourself these five questions first:

1. Why is this an inappropriate relationship? Who would categorize it in that way?

2. Who would be hurt if I go ahead with it?

3. What are the moral/legal/social implications of going ahead with it?

4. What changes will it make to my life if I follow my heart (or whichever body part is leading you)?

5. Is it really worth it?

Odds are that, when you've asked yourself these questions, you will decide that maybe it isn't such a great idea after all. However, if after seriously thinking about it you decide that it is the right thing to do, then I wish you luck. Some wonderful lifetimes have grown from 'He's too old for her', 'She's from the wrong kind of family', 'They'll never last'. But *be careful*…

CHAPTER SUMMARY
Pocket Primer – Meeting People

1. The more pressure you put on yourself, the more difficult the process will be.

2. Stay positive – you will attract what you believe is out there.

3. Stay open to all possibilities.

4. Believe in what you have to offer.

5. Be yourself – be honest and stay natural.

The biggest problem most of us have, in regards to meeting new people and starting relationships, is that we go into it with a long list of who it should be, when it should be, where it should be, and exactly how it should happen. The best thing you can do for yourself is to lose those thoughts. Love is a force like no other, with its own ideas as to when it will show up, where it will show up, and in what guise it will present itself. Leave yourself free to be surprised and I guarantee you will be.

Helping
Love Grow

" Lots of people want to ride with you in the limo, but what you want is someone who will take the bus with you when the limo breaks down. **"**

Oprah Winfrey

Chapter 3
Helping Love Grow

Before we start out, we tend to believe that the difficult bit is 'getting a partner'. That we'll 'catch' someone and the difficult bit is over. Tee-hee! It's just the beginning. A relationship is an ongoing process. We think the whole process of finding someone is a big, complicated activity and after you've 'caught' them, if it's a good relationship, it will just work out all by itself. It just isn't so. This is when the real hard work begins. Putting on a bit of lip-gloss or delivering a snappy chat-up line is easy; it's building on all this that is the challenge.

One of the secrets to a good relationship is finding two people whose wants and needs are fairly similar, and who are both willing to put in the necessary work to turn the situation from 'just dating' into a proper relationship. Keep in mind that Rome was not built in a day so don't expect the perfect relationship overnight. It might be a bit bumpy in the beginning, but the work must be done and, fingers crossed, it will be worth it.

Moving the relationship on

There comes a moment when you realize that maybe this is something more than a casual friendship. Something alters your routine and you don't see each other as often as you usually do, and you miss her like crazy. Or he mentions a new girl working in his office and you feel a stab of jealousy. Whatever the signals, you realize that you might want more from this person than you currently have. You want to take the relationship to another level.

Ask yourself the following questions:

- What kind of relationship am I looking for?

- Where do I want to end up?

- Have I gotten any signals indicating that they might feel the same as me?

Start the steps to moving the relationship on by planning an activity you've not indulged in before. Going away for a weekend, meeting your close friends, are just the kind of thing that indicates a relationship is moving into new territory. Suggest doing something at a point a couple of months away – booking tickets for an exhibition or concert – see how the suggestion is received. If there is an uncomfortable silence and flimsy excuses, then back down for the time being. If the suggestion is greeted positively, then maybe you're on the right track and there just might be a future.

Consider carefully

Take a moment to decide if you truly believe the relationship has legs. Do you want to move the relationship along because your 38th birthday is rapidly approaching, it's the best sex you've ever had, it's easier than looking for someone else, OR do you want to move the relationship along because you have very special feelings for this particular person.

Ask yourself this

Here are a few more questions to ask yourself before you make the final decision.

1. Would you say your attraction to this person is more physical than mental?

2. Is there anyone else in the world you would rather be with?

3. Do you trust this person?

4. Are you comfortable in this person's company?

5. If you close your eyes and try to imagine the rest of your life without this person, how do you feel?

Answer these questions carefully and you should end up with a very accurate portrayal of the situation.

Making your feelings known

This is the tricky bit, and what we are most afraid of, but it *has to be done*. Some people, like me, can be read like a book. If I like someone, they will know because it is written all over my face – couldn't hide it if I wanted to, believe me there have been times when I have tried. But not everyone is an open book, so you cannot sit there quietly assuming that the other person knows how deep your true feelings are. I know this is difficult. You are putting yourself on the line, opening yourself up to possible hurt, and putting yourself in the most vulnerable position possible.

It is important that you move forward at a rate you are comfortable with. Sometimes a look is worth a thousand words. Take the person's hand, look into their eyes and say *'You know I really like you'* and smile. Might sound odd, but it works. You want to open the door to a conversation, not necessarily make a grand declaration; there will be time enough for that later.

Ask him/her

This is a step for the brave, but, if you can do this, it could save you a lot of heartache down the road. It's really important that both parties are coming from the same place. You need to check that one of you isn't thinking that moving the relationship on means spending a bit more time together – while the other feels that you've stepped on the movable sidewalk that will deposit you both at the altar. You must decide what this change in circumstance means to you and the other person; for example will you continue to see other people?

" I love being married. It's so great to find that one special person you want to annoy for the rest of your life. **"**

Rita Rudner

Check your direction

It isn't about making demands or issuing ultimatums, but it is about making sure you're both heading in the same direction. In any decent relationship, there will be plateaus and rites of passage. The first time you meet a family member, the first time you go on holiday. If there are children from a previous relationship then there's the first time you're introduced to them. It isn't necessary or possible to establish, right at the beginning, what route the two of you will take. But it is important that you have a strong sense that you are both interested in going in the same direction.

When parties have different views of the situation

When someone says 'He'll come round I'm sure of it', my heart falls to the floor. Millions of relationships from the beginning of time have been based on this concept. One person states what they are expecting to do or be a part of. The other is diametrically opposed but has complete faith that it will only take time before the other party will come to their senses. Yes, people do sometimes change their mind, but usually they don't. Sometimes the person who said they really didn't ever plan on getting married really meant it. The person who said no to children might really mean it. You are setting yourself up for an almighty crash if you go into a relationship with the idea that you are going to change the other person and ignore their beliefs. Take people as you find them, if they change then you're lucky, but don't count on it. If them staying the way they are or holding on to the beliefs they currently have will cause untold difficulties, then walk away now.

Taking the next step

If you are just going to spend more time together, then there isn't really anything to be done. You might want to decide between you if you need to make a semi-official announcement to your friends. Terrible rows have come out of one person telling the world and the other wanting it to be a secret. If you are doing something as monumental as moving in together, then it is crucial that you both clearly communicate what your expectations are. Several big conversations need to be had and guidelines put in place and agreed to. This is especially important if you will be taking actions that will involve finances, but more on that in the section on money. Don't be put off, though, as this is one of the loveliest times in a new relationship. The slate is clean, everything is sparkling and shiny, and the world is your oyster.

The role of communication

If I had to choose one element that can make or break a relationship, it would be communication. The business of how we go about making our thoughts, feelings, likes, dislikes, troubles, joys, and any other emotion you can think of, known to others. How we lay out these things and how we receive them from other folk is possibly the biggest determination as to the quality of life you enjoy in any arena. But, in the area of relationships, Communication is the dealmaker or dealbreaker.

First, let's define communication. If I were to ask you what that means, many of you might say 'telling people what I think'. That is only a small part of communication. It is very important, when beginning a relationship, that you discuss your methods of communicating. If you are a shouter, then you say *'Listen, sometimes I get a bit loud but I really don't mean it. If it bothers you then let me know'*. If you're someone who holds it in *'Listen, sometimes it takes me awhile to let it out but be patient I'll get there eventually'*. I cannot stress enough just how important it is to get this right. Many a good relationship has fallen by the wayside due to poor communication; don't let yours be one of them.

The role of trust

One of the most important building blocks of any relationship is trust. It is trust in this other person that provides you with the feeling of security that most of us are looking for in a relationship. And without it, there will be that constant feeling of unease. When I ask women 'Do you trust him?' you would be surprised how many cheerfully say 'Not on your Nelly!' This isn't good and it isn't healthy.

Ask yourself this – what is it about the person that you don't trust? Do you not trust them to be faithful? Do you not trust them to be truthful? Is it money that you don't trust them about? Do you not trust them to stay with you? Is it all of the above or do you just feel that it is inevitable that they will, at some point, hurt you badly.

Watch your focus

I am now going to say something that might upset some of you – and I will repeat it throughout this book. In my experiences, both personal and professional, *you tend to get what you focus on*. If you go around expecting the worst, chances are the worst will happen. Yes, you usually cannot prove that it may not have happened if you hadn't focused on it; but do us all a favor and focus on your relationship working and working brilliantly and then go for it. *(See Forgive and Forget, page 84.)*

Choosing your battles

When most of our mothers were young, the rule of thumb was that a good wife is obedient. She listens to the head of the household (the man), she doesn't cause trouble. Things have changed, and the past couple of decades have taught us that swallowing your anger is extremely unhealthy – both for your body and your mind. However, constantly ranting and raving is also no good for anyone. It weakens your relationship and is very distressing for your children. I am constantly coming across children whose main wish is for their parents to *just stop* arguing. It makes them feel unsettled and insecure.

To argue or not to argue? – That is the question

What do you do when you are bothered? Where is the line between expressing your negative feelings in a constructive fashion and burying them? Learn how to choose your battles. Everything doesn't need to be cause for an argument. When you see something that bothers you, ask yourself 'How serious is this? Is it really worth making a fuss about?' 'Can I change my attitude about it so that it doesn't really bother me?' If you can't, then mention it but in a non-confrontational way, and don't wait until you are about to explode.

How to argue effectively

'All married couples should learn the art of battle as they should learn the art of making love. Good battle is objective and honest, never vicious or cruel. Good battle is healthy and constructive and brings to a marriage the principle of equal partnership.' Ann Landers

The make-or-break factor

How disagreements are handled within a relationship can be one of the strongest determining factors as to whether or not the relationship works in the long term. You may find that the more emotionally distant a topic, the more a man is willing to argue it. He will argue himself into a blue fit over who is the better basketball player. But try to have a conversation about how hurt your feelings were when he forgot your birthday and many a man will be as quiet as a church mouse. We women also have our issues, often tending to make mountains out of molehills.

What outcome are you looking for?

It helps if you know from the beginning what you want the outcome to be. Do you want to solve the problem, or are you just interested in having a spat? If you're letting off steam, then have your rant and say 'Right, well I just felt I needed to say that'. However, I would advise against employing this tactic with any frequency because, after a while, it could permanently damage your relationship.

Don't beat a dead horse

What if you're trying to resolve a specific issue and can see that this particular exchange is not getting anywhere, or you just don't feel like talking anymore? Then *'It seems as if we aren't making any progress on this right now, how do you feel about ending this particular conversation about it and we can pick it up again when we're both up for it?'* You have very clearly expressed your feelings that this isn't going anywhere, but that the matter has not yet been resolved and will need to be discussed further at another time.

Controlling your mood

A couple of points to keep in mind. If you really want a solution, then don't shout. Nothing inflames a situation like raised voices. Be forceful if necessary, but remain measured and calm. Don't say you're sorry if you don't mean it. That just makes you angry inside, which will eventually cause yet another argument. Too much arguing is no good, but not arguing at all can be even worse. So, if you must do it, please do it effectively, with a view to finding a solution rather than destroying your relationship.

How to make up

Don't go to sleep not speaking. If you can't resolve the issue then, after acknowledging that you're not going to take it any further at this particular point in time, *say 'Present circumstances aside, I do love you'*. Or something simpler, like *'Have a good night'*. There are some people who feel that the best way to make up from an argument is something material, like flowers or chocolates or extra sex. ☺ For some, this might work (especially the latter) but what most people, especially women, are really looking for is an indication that you genuinely regret whatever has happened.

Ways to apologize

The other party will also want an indication when you apologize, and you should, that you intend making a serious effort not to let it happen again. If talking about emotional stuff isn't easy for you, then the shops are full to overflowing with 'Roses are red violets are blue I sure am sorry I acted like poo-poo' cards. Buy one. Believe it or not, that will often work better than a very impersonal gift. If you've really pulled a big one, then plan an activity that you know will mean something to the other person. It could be something big, but you'll find that cooking his favorite dinner or running her a candlelit bath can reinforce the fact that you are sorry. Simple phrases like *'I really do appreciate you'* and *'I really am sorry'* then moving on and getting back on track with the relationship.

Talking about money

A few years ago, some research came out that said that the biggest reason couples were splitting up wasn't infidelity but finances. Granted, the research might have been commissioned by a bank but the fact is that, for a lot of the couples who come through my doors, finances, and how they are handled or mishandled, are at the center of their difficulties. It is very important that, in a relationship, no one feels like they're being treated like a child, especially in relationship to finances. It is also important that no one feels as if they're being taken advantage of.

Setting the ground rules

The tone of finances in a relationship is usually set in the very beginning. As embarrassing or difficult as it might be for some of us to discuss it, we must be clear about finances from Day One. You must state clearly, from the beginning, how you feel the finances should work, as it will cause nothing but grief down the road if you don't. Saying 'Well, actually, I wasn't comfortable with that but didn't want to say at the time' isn't going to help anyone.

" A good marriage is one which allows for change and growth in the individuals and in the way they express their love. **"**

Pearl Buck

Getting outside help

Sometimes it helps to bring a third party into the conversation. In every library, bookstore, and on Amazon, you can now find workbooks on finances. Get one. Sit down with a couple of pencils and make up a plan to order your finances. As time goes by, and your relationship grows, there will be more and more expenses and serious financial stuff to deal with. It is very important that you get into the habit of talking about it in an open fashion from the very beginning. A relationship is like building a house, it is much better to build a solid foundation at the start than to spend money later on in repairs.

The role of ex's

How easy life would be if we didn't have ex's, but the fact is that we all will have a couple of them buried somewhere in the backyard. I believe the less said about one's ex's the better. No good ever comes of it but I know as well as I am sitting here that you're not going to listen to me. I shall say 'Talk at your own peril'. It will be a rare man or woman who can overcome the urge, in the middle of an argument, to say 'No wonder he left you' or 'That woman you've been calling crazy wasn't crazy at all, you really are a codependent mama's boy'.

Discussing your past relationships

While I strongly believe that you shouldn't volunteer information on your past relationships, I also believe that you shouldn't lie. 'So what did your last relationship die of?' – *Really* Bad Answer: *'He cheated on me with my best friend. I always used to tell him that I thought he would cheat on me, and he did. I was glad to see the back of him because he was rubbish in bed and, anyway, he didn't want to get married or have children so what use was he?'* Really Good Answer: *'We just had different paths in mind and thought it better that we go our separate ways. Anyway, this quiche really is tasty where did you buy it?'* I suspect that there's not a snowball in hell's chance that you're going to do the latter but, for my sake, can we aim for somewhere in-between the two?

Dealing with jealousy

Other issues of ex's can be things like your new partner being jealous of the past relationship, the amount of time you still spend with the ex, or if they have the feeling that you're still not completely clear of the relationship and there is a chance you will go back to the person. Hand on heart, is there cause for worry? If not, then here are a couple of things you can do.

1. Ask your new partner what it is they are afraid of? 'That isn't going to happen because I am with you now. Don't forget that I broke up with them before I met you and already knew beyond a shadow of doubt that the relationship was over.'

2. Make a list of the things you prefer about your new love and tell them what they are 'Sam was OK but you're fabulous because a-b-c... I am so happy to be with you because I've always wanted to be with someone who could build a fire by rubbing two sticks together.'

Topics to avoid

I happen to believe that a *tiny* bit of jealousy can be healthy. But if this person starts trying to control your behavior, then watch out; this inclination to control you might rear its ugly head in other areas as well. Men – here's a tip: *never* EVER answer questions about an ex's appearance and, if possible, I would also avoid showing photographs. There is nothing more competitive than a woman. Many a tear has been shed 'She's way more beautiful than me, he'll never stay with me after being with someone who looks like her, etc. etc. etc.' And boys don't be fooled! Any question, however innocent, really translates to 'Was she prettier, sexier, had a bigger bust/smaller bum than me?' Don't fall for it! Ladies – under *no* circumstance answer any sex questions about your previous relationships. 'It was ok/alright' is the only appropriate answer.

The distinction between ex-partner and mother/father-of-my-child

There is usually a marked difference in how one reacts to this issue if you yourself have previously been married. You will tend to be more reasonable about the expectations of your new partner's former partner. You know that no matter what the current circumstances are between you and your new partner, they will always be tied together with their ex as parents of their children. Sometimes it is very difficult for single people to understand this so, if you're a parent and your new partner has never been one, then it is important that you have a conversation about your role as a parent. Often people get confused and think that the constant visits to the house where your children live means that you are still deeply in love with their mother.

Clarifying your role as a parent

You must lay your cards on the table with your new partner; *'Emily and I aren't together anymore because we were just not right for each other BUT I am still a hands-on father to Bobby and Susannah. I see them every Sunday afternoon and on holidays. I will try my best not to let it crowd our relationship but they are my kids and I am very committed to them.'* You've laid your cards on the table and, chances are, you will have made a good impression with your new girl. If, however, she doesn't understand or kicks up a fuss, it's for you to decide, but I would find such an attitude a cause for concern.

When you're a mother

If you're a mother and in a new relationship, then your issues are twofold. There is the 'When do I introduce him to the idea of the children?' 'When do I introduce the children to the idea of him?' I'm sure I don't need to tell you not to hide the fact that you have children. If you were the sort of person who would do that then you probably wouldn't be reading this book. But just in case – do NOT under any circumstance do that. Many a man has gotten up from the table and walked away, not because a woman has children but because she lied about it. Mention quite quickly that you have two children; but don't talk about them constantly; there'll be time enough for that later. Give the relationship a chance to grow first.

Dealing with a difficult ex

If either of you gets stuck with a difficult ex then you do have my sympathies. What you do about it depends on how you see the future of your current relationship. I have known of women who have taken difficult ex's out for coffee and given the *'Your children are really wonderful, you are so lucky to have them; anything I can do to help make your job easier please let me know. They will always only have one mother and I respect that'* speech. I've yet to hear an instance when it didn't have the desired effect.

Communication between your new partner and their children

You should never restrict the communication between a parent and their children. But if you have the sense that the parent/ex is just trying to cause disruption, then it is completely within your right to say so. If you find that the parent is calling three or four times a night and being demanding on your current partner then it might be necessary to have the *'Do you mind asking her, whenever possible, to call during the day or between 7 and 7.30 or 10 and 10.30'* conversation.

Family structures in our modern world

As all types of extended-family relationships become more common, we seem to be coming up with more effective ways of handling them. I am constantly meeting families where you can't figure out where the 'old' children end and the 'new' begin. And have been to several dinners where 'Oh and this is the mother of Ella and Samuel…' and no one bats an eyelash. It can be done and is best for all concerned.

The role of your family

This can depend on how old you are, your background or your relationship with your family. It can also depend on the nature of your relationship and where you see it heading.

The role of your new partner's family

When I was young, free, and single, I had no thoughts one way or another as to what someone's family was like. When I got a bit older and started thinking of building a proper relationship with someone their family then became a very important part of the equation. What sort of relationship did they have with their family? How much input did their family have in their day to day lives? Were there things about the other person's family that might impact on our relationship, such as religious differences, etc? To some people these things don't matter at all. I have to say that to me they did. I wasn't willing to marry into a family where the difference in our backgrounds could possibly cause a problem for our children. Times have moved on since then and those kinds of issues are usually less of a worry than they were; unless you come from a family that strictly observes certain religious guidelines.

Parents who think their offspring are still children

Nowadays you're more likely to have problems with an overprotective father who thinks no one is good enough for his little princess – even if said princess is 38. And, of course, the mother who feels that no Mazda-driving smart-aleck career woman (who has probably slept with half of Oklahoma) is going to iron her son's socks with the same attention to detail that she has for the past 40 years, never mind raise her precious grandchildren in accordance with her rules. How you respond to all this will often depend on what kind of family you come from.

Mothers-in-law, handle with care

One of my closest friends is now dealing with a mother-in-law from hell and I swear I don't know how she hasn't throttled the woman. On the other hand, I have to say that my ex mother-in-law is an angel from heaven and we remain firm friends, so don't always expect a mother-in-law to be the enemy. Usually she is just a woman who wants the best for her son so take a deep breath and smile.

Dealing with siblings

As far as siblings go, try not to get involved in historical scraps – remain neutral, it's safer. Try not to drag someone away from their family, but if there are aspects of the situation that you are uncomfortable with, then feel free to say so. You are all adults and entitled to start your own life. I always suggest staying quietly on the outskirts of a new family in the early days and step in slowly and carefully – that's the safest way.

Marriage/Commitment

*For the sake of ease, I am going to refer to everything in this section as 'marriage'.

'If one professes a disinclination for marriage, I only set it down that they have not yet seen the right person.' Jane Austen

The difference between a marriage and a wedding

If we're going to talk about marriage then let us first be clear that getting married is one thing – having a wedding is another. If having a wedding is the reason you're even thinking of this, then for the love of Pete drop the idea *immediately!* A wedding is a party that lasts for only a few hours and the fun is over once you take the dress off. 'A husband is for life not just for Christmas' so act accordingly.

The legal benefits of getting hitched

Folk who are against marriage will often say 'It's only a bit of paper' or 'We don't like society telling us what to do'. Yet these are often the same people who complain that they don't have the same rights as married folk. I once had to do some research into the history of marriage and discovered, to my surprise, that marriage was not introduced because people were falling in love, or because the church said you had to – that all came later. The original purpose of marriage was to have a framework by which to disentangle unions if they went awry. That is why it used to only be rich folk who got married; and you didn't want some errant son-in-law keeping the half of Leicestershire you had given him as a wedding present. So 'that bit of paper' is invaluable if you sadly come to disentangle your union, as many cohabiting couples have now found out. Never mind unmarried fathers who sadly, legally, have little or no rights at all.

Shed the fear and take the chance

But let's not dwell on the negative. 'What if it doesn't work out?' Where would we be as a civilization if we never tried anything because we were afraid it might fail? However, don't get married if you feel it guarantees you exemption from loneliness, money worries, or a childless future – it doesn't. Get married because you're not afraid of commitment and even more importantly if you're not afraid of failure.

CHAPTER SUMMARY
Pocket Primer – Communication

1. **Get in the habit of saying positive things.** Some of us only open our mouths when we have something negative to say.

2. **Do not discuss your issues with** everyone else before discussing them with the person in question. And, if for some reason you decide to ignore this advice, then please, please do not say 'Well I was talking to my mother about it and she thinks…' That is almost guaranteed to turn it from communication to argument.

3. **Don't be impatient.** Who knows how long it has taken the person initiating the conversation to begin. You care about this person and whatever they are about to say is probably, in their mind, for the good of the relationship.

4. If you don't understand what is being said to you or what the issue is, then **ask for clarification.**

5. **Choose your times carefully.** Ladies, this does not mean right when he's about to fall asleep. Gentlemen, this does not mean while she is changing a nappy, looking for her briefcase, curling her eyelashes AND feeding the dog.

6. If you are the person initiating the conversation then be sure to **let the other person have their say as well.**

7. **Listen carefully to their response.** You might find it changes your perception of the issue.

8. Women tend to respond more intensely to tone and volume so **men please watch both.** On the other hand, men tend to process information in short groups of words so **ladies don't waffle on.** Ten words and get to the point. Stop, let them absorb – then deliver another ten words.

9. **Acknowledge the effort** the person has made to start this conversation. 'I know it must have been difficult for you to say this and I appreciate it.' And if you also feel 'I'm not sure if I agree but I'll take on board what you've said', then feel free to say so.

    If you're the person who started the conversation then 'Thank you for listening so patiently, I really needed to get this off my chest'.

10. **Speak regularly and often.** You would be surprised how little many couples talk these days. There is always one survey or another saying that it is six minutes a day, or some other horrifying figure. Lack of communication is one of the saddest things you often hear as a reason for couples drifting apart.

    Make a point of having even a short chat each day about something you want rather than have to talk about. Sounds simplistic but in the long run it's the little things that count.

Marriage isn't about trying to find the person you fancy the most then closing your eyes and hoping the feeling lasts for the rest of your life. That is a ridiculous and impractical expectation. Love grows and changes, and that subtle difference you feel when you get married is due to its ebb and flow; the growth of an ever-strengthening bond. Like the tide, there are times when you will think love has drained away and then it will come flowing back and is all the sweeter for its return. One day, hopefully, you will find the person who, when you close your eyes and try to imagine the rest of your life without them – you just can't. That is the feeling you're looking for. Then and only then is it the right time to say 'I do' and know you'll really mean it. There are no foolproof choices you can make in this life but, if you truly believe, go for it.

" Don't smother each other. No one can grow in the shade. **"**

Leo Buscaglia

Keeping Love Alive

" Love is not enough. It must be the foundation, the cornerstone – but not the complete structure. It is much too pliable, too yielding. "

Bette Davis

Chapter 4
Keeping Love Alive

You've made the commitment. You've walked down the aisle, gotten the mortgage, bought a dog, signed up for a family membership at the gym – or done whatever counts for a solid commitment in your world. You've hitched your pony to this person's wagon and the plan is most likely this is it – you'll be two old folk sitting on the bench in the park holding hands and sharing a bag of M&M's.

How do you get from here to there? Are there steps you can take to guarantee that you'll end up with matching "I'm With Stupid" t-shirts? I wish there was but sadly there are no guaranteed Ten Steps To Forever Together and it takes more than just wanting it to reach the finish line. Whenever I talk to couples who have been together forever, the one thing they will always say is 'It takes work but it's worth it'. In other words, you do have to make an effort; but if you do the work there is a good chance you'll reap the rewards.

Conversely, if you don't do the work, if you just sit there and think it will 'just happen' then don't be surprised with the results. That would be like planting a seedling, never watering it, then complaining when it doesn't grow into a tree.

Building on your dreams

1. Dedicate yourself to the relationship.

2. Don't willingly do things that you know will harm the relationship. It takes work, effort and maintenance.

3. Know each other's likes and dislikes.

4. Know what makes each other happy or sad.

5. Be loyal to each other.

6. Give each other the freedom and time in which to maintain your individuality. Two wholes make a better unit.

7. Make sure the balance of power within the relationship regularly flows back and forth.

8. Do not treat each other with disrespect.

9. Take the extra time and make the extra effort to understand each other.

10. Take a minute each and every day to look each other in the eyes and say 'I love you'.

Keeping the relationship fresh

Did you know that being in love is actually an altered chemical state? Well it is. Many of us will experience clammy hands, racing pulse, butterflies in our tummies, and all sorts. Dopamine, Norepinephrine and Serotonin are the culprits that can have you obsessing over the object of your affection, planning to give up your job and move you both to a desert island, all and every form of insanity. You may also find yourself feeling disconnected when not in sight of your one true love. The good news is that this state of madness usually lasts for about 6-9 months. The bad news is that a lot of us expect it to last forever and, when it ends, we think the relationship is over.

Moving from lust to love

The truth of it is that, in many ways, this is when the relationship really begins. This is when we go from attraction to attachment, and it is attachment that will keep your relationship together. The chemicals your brain releases at this stage are oxytocin and vasopressin. Sadly, they're not to be found in aisle 7 at the local pharmacy so it's not going to be possible to sprinkle a few vials over your partner's cornflakes and sit back. If you pay close attention to the pointers listed above, you will be well ahead of the game, but I want you to be realistic.

Attachment – the holy grail of a relationship

Keep in mind that trying to feel the way you felt in the first couple of months for the rest of your lives is not practical. That is a primeval mating instinct that we were born with, so that we would be attracted to each other, procreate, and move on. However, the stage where you now are might have fewer fireworks but should provide you with the incomparable feeling of being loved for who you are. Creating and maintaining attachment is the secret to maintaining the healthy state of the relationship.

Making an effort (why)

How many times have you heard others, or maybe even said yourself, 'I woke up one day and I was living with a stranger'? And how many times has that phrase been the first gong in the death march of the relationship? Call it boredom; call it the loss of love; the fact of the matter is that this situation is usually down to at least one party no longer making the effort needed to keep a relationship ticking over. Usually, it hasn't been a conscious decision – 'I can't be bothered anymore, let the chips fall where they may'. It just sets in like damp or dry rot and once it sets in it is hell and all to get rid of it – and you'll always worry about it coming back. So that's why you make an effort – an ounce of prevention is worth a pound of cure.

Making an effort (how)

Remember the chemical reactions we talked about earlier? The oxy-whatsits and the neo-doodah? Here's the thing – once they set in, they tend to grow. In other words, getting into the habit of making an effort makes it second nature; which then makes it a routine; which then makes it less of a big deal. The attachment grows and the more attached you become to each other the more you feel the need to reach out and maintain the attachment.

1. **Touching.** Touch your partner frequently, and not necessarily in a sexual way. Oxytocin is sometimes called 'the cuddle chemical'.

2. **Listen to each other.** People feel valued when they're listened to.

3. **Make eye contact with each other.** Sounds simple, but you would be surprised how we are sometimes having a conversation while reading the paper, ironing, or staring at the telly.

4. Stop what you're doing and **properly greet each other** at the end of the day.

5. **Hold hands** when you're sleeping.

6. Get in the habit of **doing new things** together.

7. **Date each other.** Once a month, without fail, go on a proper date. No kids. Nice clothes. Away from the house.

8. **Have dreams and goals** and work towards them. Doesn't matter how small they are. Saving $100 for a double massage session. Build a birdcage together. Doesn't matter what it is as long as it is something that you will dream together, plan together, and work on with each other.

9. **Compliment each other** regularly.

10. **Surprise each other** with little things. Tuck her favorite chocolate bar in her purse. Book him a test-drive in his dream car.

I know it all sounds like a lot of work, but isn't your happiness worth it?

“ Trouble is part of your life and if you don't share it you don't give the person who loves you a chance to love you enough. **”**

Dinah Shore

Spending time together

This tends to be more of an issue in relationships where children are involved. Your natural instinct might be to put your children first, and while they are your priority, so is your relationship. You can do both – give your children what they need and keep the relationship between you and your partner alive. But it does takes planning.

The role of the clock in your relationship

With the best will in the world, there are only 24 hours in a day. Work, children, day to day practicalities and by the time you're finished there's precious little time or energy left for your relationship. Yes you are both in the same boat but there are often gender differences as to how this situation is regarded. Women often feel 'We're both in the same situation' and assume that the man understands. Men often feel 'She's only interested in the children, what about me?' This is a serious dilemma and often, when you sit down with a couple in crisis, the lack of quality time spent together will be cited as the reason behind the demise of the relationship.

Making time for the two of you

Without careful attention, you run the risk of totally losing sight of each other. This is another reason why suggestions in the **Making an effort (how)** section *(pages 73-74)* are so important. Keeping each other within easy reach is a lot easier than trying to reach across the Grand Canyon.

The one minute that will save your relationship

Be it one minute a day or one week a year – give each other some Us Time – it isn't a luxury, it's a necessity.

Spotting trouble and nipping it in the bud

One of the most important habits you should get into is talking through issues as they come up. This does NOT mean nagging. It doesn't mean constantly finding fault or complaining. But it does mean having a proper, non-parental, non-judgemental discussion when there is a problem. If something is important, then ignoring it will not make it disappear. In fact, ignoring it will usually just make it grow bigger and more difficult to deal with.

Don't stick your head in the sand

If you are paying attention to the state of your relationship, you will usually be aware when something is not right. Please don't fall into the habit of calling your mother or your girlfriends 'Something's wrong with Alan, what do you think it is?' If you want to know what's wrong with Alan then, errrrm, ask Alan. A simple 'Are you OK? You seem a bit distracted/quiet/sad/down lately, is there anything I can do?' – lets the person know that you have noticed that something is off and you're there if they want to talk. If the person's behavior has changed radically, then ask yourself 'Has she always done that and I've just never noticed it?' If you can definitely say that it is new behavior and you're not comfortable with it, then 'I notice that you've been staying out with the people from the office a lot lately, is something wrong and would you like to talk about it?'

Solving problems

There are times in even the best of relationships when you come upon stumbling blocks. It could be anything from you wanting a holiday in Hawaii and he wants a new sports car to she doesn't want to have another child and you do. While how you communicate can be the make or break factor in your relationship, so can how you problem-solve. Because of this, it is good to have a problem-solving strategy in place and to use it for anything from 'I want to change the wallpaper' to 'Should we move to Florida?'

1. **Identify the problem.** If the problem is a big one, it will be easy to identify. But sometimes the problem is 'just a feeling' – in which case you might need to sit down and give it some thought.

2. **Create some possible solutions.** Try to come up with one or two possible solutions, don't come to the table empty-handed. You will want to solve the problem together, not just dump it on the other person.

3. **Construct a proper time to sit down and talk about it.** I cannot repeat enough times that it is often not what you've said but how and when you say it that determines whether or not you have a successful outcome.

4. **Get their opinion on the situation.** How many times have I heard 'Well she didn't really care what I thought, she had it all worked out so I didn't even bother to comment'? At each step of the way, ask their opinion. Step One: 'I've been thinking about *x*, *y*, *z* and the more I think about it, the more I realize what a big problem it is. Do you agree?' Step Two: 'I don't know how we could go about solving it, I was thinking that maybe we could try *a*, or *b* but I'm not sure. What do you think of those ideas? Or do you have any ideas that you think might work better?'

If solving the problem is going to involve investigating certain possibilities, then suggest that you do it together, 'Let's go on the internet and see what we can find', 'How about we make an appointment at the bank for next week and go in and speak to someone?' Sharing the responsibility for solving big problems is one of the most important building blocks of a successful relationship.

Keeping up appearances

This section should really be called 'elbows off the table, tracksuit bottoms in the bin'. When you talk to women about the state of their relationship, they will often cite the change in their partner's behavior as cause for concern. When you talk to men about the state of their relationship, they will often cite the state of their partner's appearance as their cause for concern. Yes, sometimes the appearance or behavior has definitely changed, but quite often, if we're honest with ourselves, we've just stopped making the effort. It's easier to haul on the tracksuit bottoms to do the grocery shopping or when you come in from a hard day in the office. And guys, you know she loves you so leaving the toilet seat up or commenting loudly on bodily functions should be one of the benefits of settledom should it not? Well, not really. So try to make a bit of effort, both of you, you'll feel all the better for it.

The role of romance

Let's start this topic by clearing up two of the most widely held misconceptions. Ladies – romance is not only something that boys do for girls – enjoying romance is not gender specific. Gentlemen – romance is not necessarily expensive and is definitely not always a precursor to sexual activity. Women are always complaining to me that their men are not romantic. Then I ask 'When was the last time you did something romantic for him?' I get a blank look and sometimes even a 'We don't have to do it for them, they're supposed to do it for us!' Oh really? I must have missed that page in the rule book then. And boys, why is it that when your women ask you to do something romantic you so often choose Option A – flowers from the gas station, or Option B – something involving red lace.

We both like it, we both need it

OK, both of you listen up. True Romance is equally important to both sexes and whilst it often leads to sex, it doesn't have to. In ancient times, marriages were usually arranged and were primarily business relationships based on property, money, or political alliances. Then, in medieval times, the importance of romance in relationship to marriage came into the picture so that troubadours and poets could run a brisk trade in soppy songs and poems. It's been downhill ever since.

66 A successful marriage
requires falling in love
many times, always with
the same person. **99**

Mignon McLaughlin

How to be romantic (even if you've never been before)

Do you want to know what the secret to romance is? **Romance is something that you do or say to your loved one that no one else could do or say and have the same meaning.** Here's an example. You buy her a giant diamond ring from Tiffany's that's *very nice*. You buy her the same diamond ring and bury it in a can of baked beans, because that was the first thing she ever cooked for you – *that is romantic.* You can buy her the latest bottle of designer perfume, or you can make her a compilation CD of her favorite songs. You can rent his favorite DVD (even if it is *Die Hard 17*), cook his favorite meal (even if it's Polish sausage and key lime pie) *that is romantic.* And when they say 'You remembered…' you know you have a result!

Talking about s-e-x

In our current climate, where 5-year-olds are being taught about the birds and the bees and we know the intimate details of our politician's' sex lives, it is difficult to believe that we still have difficulties talking about sex. Why is that, you might wonder. When our grandparents were younger, sex was a very private matter. You might be aware that you weren't being satisfied. You might wish that the person on top (or underneath) you didn't just lie there pretending you were James Bond – but you certainly weren't going to say anything. You might know something was missing but you could only guess at what it was.

Why you must talk if there is a problem

Nowadays, everywhere you turn there is an article telling you exactly, and with great detail, what should be happening to you. Billboards and tv adverts will show you the wonderful sexual experiences you are missing if you're not using the right dandruff shampoo or driving the right car. You might think that this constant exposure and over-familiarization with matters sexual would make it easy for us to discuss, but for most of us it hasn't. In fact, for a fair few of us, it is even more difficult. But if it is an issue in your relationship then discuss it you must.

Starting the conversation

Sex within a relationship is a very sensitive subject indeed and needs to be approached carefully. Some people seem to find it easier to tell a total stranger 'I prefer when you do it *this* way' than to say the same thing to someone with whom they are in a committed relationship. You may be worrying that you might hurt their feelings, you might just not know how to say it, you might be shy, but here are some tips. Compliment the current state of play 'I love the way it feels when you do that' (if you're brave you can say what 'that' entails). Then follow that by 'Is there anything special you would like me to do?' If there is a particular move that your partner thinks makes them the king or queen of the bedroom and it makes you want to run screeching, then a simple 'You know I love it when you do *x* but I am kind of less fond of *y*. Is there anything I do that you'd prefer I didn't do?' At the end of the experience 'I really did enjoy that'.

Getting wild if you want to

If your issues involve wanting to broaden your horizons, go to the nearest bookstore and look through the shelves. There are dozens of books that you and partner can go through together, in fact, consider making a night of it. Go to the bookstore, choose a book or two, have a bottle of wine chilling, then go home and see what comes up.

Caught red-handed

It isn't my job to read you the riot act on the level of morality you should display if you are trying to keep your relationship healthy; commonsense should tell you to behave yourself. But we're not all angels and there are few relationships out there that don't have one or two rainy days, often revolving around someone getting caught with their hand in the cookie jar. That could mean anything from spending half the household budget on shoes to sleeping with someone's sibling. Now here's an interesting thing that I have gleaned from my years of agony aunting and counseling folk. Men tend to get caught, women don't. I'll give you a couple of minutes to digest that…

Bad behavior gender differences

Now let me tell you why I think that is so. If a man finds himself in a relationship where he is not happy, he will often behave badly in an attempt to get you to 'relieve him of his responsibilities'. Many times, when a man starts playing away from home or is exhibiting one or another sort of inappropriate behavior, it is the proverbial cry for help or cry for freedom. With women, usually whatever the misbehavior entails is either something they *really* want to do (like buy the shoes), or they have convinced themselves that they are deeply in love with someone, but they feel their familial responsibilities are too precious to abandon. So whatever they do they plan and execute it in such a way that discovery is not a necessary part of the situation.

Someone's been 'naughty'; someone is now **very** sorry!

1. **Be honest.** If you are confronted, then admit to your misdemeanor. If you want to hold onto your relationship then you must attempt to wipe the slate clean. Lies on top of bad behavior are never a good idea.

2. **Be brief.** The wronged party might demand a lot of detail; it is usually wise to discourage this. 'The shoes were only $200 and they're usually $500' is one thing; 'I did it because I thought he would be better in bed and he has a lot of money' is another.

3. **Allow the other person the space to vent their feelings** (as long as it is not physical – that is never acceptable). If there are children then the discussion needs to be had either away from the house or the children need to be shipped off somewhere. Please do not think that they're asleep so they won't hear, or that they are too young and they won't understand. I have worked with too many traumatized adults

now in their 30s and still wondering what made Mummy sleep with Uncle Bernie.

4. **Don't make promises you have no intention of keeping.**

5. **Say you're sorry and really mean it.** You may not regret whatever your action was, but chances are you really are sorry to have hurt your loved one and you must say so.

Forgive and Forget

Many moons ago, some bright spark decided that the word Forgive needed to be permanently attached to the word Forget. Forgive 'n' Forget became the Peanut Butter and Jelly in the world of relationships, romantic or otherwise. So let's understand something right now.

Which is possible – which is not

It is possible, and relatively within the range of accomplishment (don't want to say 'easy') to forgive. But the only things one forgets are where you put the car keys and what day is her birthday? This is a very, very important thing to know when involved in a long-term relationship, and the earlier in the relationship you master the technique, the stronger your chances of survival and success. Here's the deal – first you forgive; which translates to 'deal with the information in a healthy fashion'. Then you put it away neatly.

Learning to forgive

Step 1. Try, if possible, to understand what happened and why.

Step 2. Let it be known that you were hurt/angry/saddened by what happened.

Step 3. Express your feelings about how you would react if the situation were to be repeated.

Step 4. Put it in a box up on a shelf.

" Tis the most tender part of love, each other to forgive. **"**

John Sheffield

Leave the sore tooth alone

Don't try to bury it or burn it; that gives it power to come back and haunt you. It follows the 'don't think about carrots' rule. You'll think about nothing but. Better you take away the power that the thought has, then it is less likely to come back and haunt you. You know the tooth is sore, don't poke it.

How not to be haunted by bad memories

This technique is very difficult, I am not going to tell you otherwise. It takes practice and faith that it will work and, after a while, like most of the stuff we are talking about, it becomes a way of life. It took me about a year to get it right, but I know some of you will be much cleverer than I at getting the hang of it. Once I got the hang of it, I even went back and applied the technique to lots of old monsters that were lurking around in the nooks and crannies of my mind. Managed to clear out a whole lot of rubbish and felt all the better for it.

Why DIY is worth it

None of us are angels and though we live in an 'it's broken, don't fix it just bin it' society, that's not really the way to go. It probably took quite a while to find this person and, before you walk away, you owe it to yourself to do whatever you can to make it work.

CHAPTER SUMMARY
Pocket Primer – S.C.R.T.S.
to a successful relationship

Sharing. Caring. Respect. Trust. Support

'Who knew it would be this difficult?' is what people now say after a half-hearted attempt is made at anything from a new diet, an exercise program, or a relationship. Why do we no longer really try to make things work? Our Instant Gratification culture has us so brainwashed that, if we don't immediately lose those ten pounds, have the skin of a 9-year-old, or the life of the fantasy couple of the moment, then bin it. Whatever it is or whoever it is. We were the 'anything is possible generation' and now so many of us are the 'can't be bothered to make a proper effort' generation.

We want Instant Perfection in a can – and it doesn't exist. This is one of the reasons our divorce rate is what it is; and has a lot to do with why so many of us are miserable. Take a look around your life, at your unread self-help books (we all have them). I have a house full of use-this-and-you-don't-need-to-go-to-the-gym gadgets. The operative words are 'use this' not 'keep it in the back of the cupboard and it will work miracles from there'. Bin a relationship too easily and you might find yourself looking back later in life, when it's too late, realizing that with a little bit of work it really would have been the one.

If Love Ends

" Every instance of heartbreak can teach us powerful lessons about creating the kind of love we really want. "

Martha Beck

Chapter 5
If Love Ends

Any real relationship will have its peaks and valleys. The minute we see a dip in the flames of passion, many of us will be convinced that 'It's finished! When will I ever learn?' But a proper relationship is like a seedling that needs constant tending to grow into a mighty oak tree. However, the day might come when you have done everything you can think of to save your relationship. It seems like you're trying to put out a forest fire with a teapot – yes, you may indeed be in trouble. There have been sessions with a counselor, a weekend in Miami – still nothing.

When you try to talk it through, it seems as though you're repeatedly banging your head on the pavement. Your conversations never resolve anything and just go round and round and you end up feeling frustrated and confused. Any discussion lasting longer than a few minutes has the potential to end up in a shouting match. What else can one say?

Maybe it really is time to move on.

Just check, double-check, and triple-check that you've tried everything because these days a good love is hard to find. If you make it through a rough patch, you will often find your relationship stronger and greatly improved. Sometimes there will be a spectacular view you've not seen before right on the other side of the valley you're currently in.

No way to go but out

There are basically two ways that a relationship ends; either with a big bang or a whimper.

BIG BANG – something happens that is too big to move beyond. You have discussed it, you've possibly forgiven or maybe you can't – whatever the reason, you've come to the end of the road and wild horses couldn't keep you from packing your bags. Maybe your anger is at a level that you cannot return from, or worse, maybe you've frozen cold. Whatever the emotional temperature, there is no light at the end of the tunnel full-stop.

WHIMPER – are you finding that together you laugh a lot less than you used to? Has the frequency and quality of your sex life changed dramatically? Do you find yourself arguing more and listening less? Are you less interested in each other's lives? Do you spend more time daydreaming about good times past rather than enjoying any good times present? Think about the two of you five years from now. What do you see and how does it make you feel?

One last thing before you leave

I would be remiss in my duties if I didn't give you a bit of advice. Whether or not you want to hear it probably depends on whether you regard the demise of your relationship as Big Bang or Whimper. Here we go…

Before you end it, why not try to get an impartial observer to take a look at the situation and see if there is anything that can be done to save the relationship. There are as many different types of help as there are relationships. There are relationship counselors. Agony aunts. If you're religious, you can go to your vicar, priest, imam, rabbi or whatever the head of your religious organization is called. Whichever avenue you choose, counseling basically has three stages.

Stage One: both parties get the opportunity to put forth their perception of the situation. What has happened to date and how you would like to see the situation change.

Stage Two: the counselor/impartial observer will help clarify why these issues are causing difficulty in the relationship – without laying the blame at either door.

Stage Three: then he or she will help you both identify the pluses and minuses of your relationship, and help you come up with possible strategies for repairing and strengthening the situation. While there is no guarantee that it will work, most people feel that it helps with either the state of the relationship or dealing with the aftermath.

Making the decision

OK, are you sure about this? Have you thought it through carefully? Is there a specific problem and, if so, have you tried to solve it? What are the ramifications of this break-up? Are there children involved, shared property, etc? While it is human nature for most people to want to discuss major events in their lives, please be careful about how, who, when, and where you discuss this issue with others.

I have known of many instances where people who were only toying with the idea of ending a relationship, shared their thoughts with one too many people and lo and behold ended up having the decision made for them. Ending up on the wrong end of an 'I heard you were about to break it off with me so let me save you the trouble' kind of conversation is not a nice place to be.

Making a difficult decision easier

Before you get to the 'discussing it with all and sundry' stage there is something you might want to try. It is one of my personal favorite life tools and can be used in just about any kind of decision making process.

It is called A Ben Franklin Balance Sheet. Take a piece of paper and divide it into two halves. Across the top of the left hand column write 'Pros' and across the top of the right hand column write 'Cons'. Then let your mind flow naturally. You will find that it is like your pen has a mind of its own. Don't stop to think about what you're writing, how many you're writing or if you're sure you really want to write it down. No one but you will ever see this list (by the way that's an order not a request) and whether or not it does what it is supposed to will be totally dependent on your honesty and free hand. Allocate yourself at least 15 minutes for this and I tell you it will be 15 minutes well spent. Usually, when you sit back and look at the paper in its entirety, the answer to your question is clear as day. By the way, this technique works for everything from what color to paint the bathroom to 'should I stay or should I go'.

Breaking up

You've realized that there was a problem. You've discussed it with your partner. You've been to counseling. You've done your Ben Franklin Balance Sheet and realized there were more Cons than Pros so it is the end and it must be said.

No texting. No emails. No cards. 'I never expected to find myself saying this, but I think it might be better if we went our separate ways. We have had a wonderful time together but for the past two years I have become more and more unhappy, and if I am this unhappy, I suspect you are as well. We've both made an effort and tried to improve things, but I think this is as good as it's going to get and this isn't enough for me. We both deserve to be happier than we are now. I would like to hope, after all we've been through, that we would wish only the best for each other'…

Two things to remember

There are two important things to keep in mind.

1.   **This too shall pass.** As badly as you may feel now, and as impossible

as it may be to believe – you will not always feel the way you feel now. The sun will shine again, or the birds sing, or whatever passes for indications of happiness in your world.

2. When something dreadful happens in your life **it is only a wasted experience if you learn nothing from it.** No matter how awful the situation, there is always something to be gained. It could improve your approach to relationships and the way you live your life. Make sure you find some way to use what has transpired towards improving your future.

Dealing with practicalities

Whatever the length or intensity of the relationship, there are going to be practicalities that need to be dealt with. Anything from who gets the Tom Jones CD to who gets the dog. If you don't live under the same roof, then gather together anything around the house that might belong to the other person. Let them know that you have their things ready for collection and, if possible, could they please gather anything of yours so you can arrange an exchange. If it is too painful, then send a courier or enlist a kind friend. However upset you might be, please don't throw all the stuff in a trash bag and resist the urge to cut the sleeves off his suits or anything similarly childish. It might bring some temporary relief but, in the long run, you will most likely regret it.

If you have been living under the same roof then it gets hugely more complicated and there is a list of things that need to be attended to. *(Children will be dealt with later, starting on page 101.)*

1. Who is going to move out?

2. What is a reasonable amount of time in which this should be accomplished? If the situation is intolerable, then one of you might move out temporarily and stay with a friend. Be sure to check the legalities of this before doing so as there are certain instances where moving out could possibly affect your rights.

3. Make a schedule for moving out.

4. Make a list of any financial obligations that are shared or pertain to the property, and determine how they are going to be handled.

5. Check schedules to see if there are any issues that need to be addressed, like pre-booked holidays, family occasions, etc. And decide how these situations should be dealt with.

6. Get all the papers together pertaining to things like mortgages, insurance, vehicle ownership, etc. Go through them, writing up a schedule for how they are going to be handled in the interim. Photocopy the papers so that you each have a file. If you are getting divorced then be sure to discuss all of the above and do not agree to anything without first discussing it with either of your attorneys.

7. Set a timetable for when all the practicalities will be sorted out.

Telling the world

An entire industry now exists around notifying people about the end of your relationship. With our usual modern attitude of 'making the best of a bad situation' there are announcement cards, parties; there are even round-robin e-cards!

Saving your emotional energy for the important things

At times like this, the world can be divided into two halves – those who you want to tell because they will really care; and those who need to be told even if it is just to keep the gossip to a dull roar. I have to say that from experience I think you have enough to deal with without having to answer a lot of questions that are either painful or no one's business. Those people with whom you are genuinely close to will have a conversation with you if and when you are ready. The rest of them can discuss it amongst themselves.

66 Divorce is the psychological equivalent of a triple coronary by-pass. Following such a monumental assault on the heart, it takes years to amend all the habits that led up to it. **99**

Mary Kay Blakely

Spreading the word

It is now perfectly acceptable to send an email or do a change-of-address card: 'As of March 1st, 2008, Robert Williams, originally of 3 Mandeville Road, Cleveland, Ohio, will be residing at 48 Twizzlehurst Lane, Kennebunkport, Maine. Any correspondence, business or personal, should be directed to that address. The cell number remains the same'. This can be sent to anyone from utility companies to your doctor and the people at the golf club; from close friends (you can write 'call me' on the bottom) to not-so-close friends. There is nothing worse than bumping into folk who don't know yet and having to tell them in the frozen food aisle at K-Mart – trust me on that one.

Telling the family

Close family should not be on the 'change of address' list. And, needless to say, close family should be told before 'the world'. How this is handled depends on a couple of things: does your family live next door or in Alaska? The circumstances of the situation, is it acrimonious or terribly civilized? I have known people who have invited both their families over and said 'There's something Bob and I want you to know…' I've known people who have written 'Dear Mom and Dad it is with great sadness that I write to tell you that it looks like Bob and I are going to go our separate ways'.

Putting into words

Personally, I would say that if you can, you should sit down with a cup of tea and a biscuit and tell them in person. For the sake of your own emotional stability, I suggest deciding in advance what you want to say 'I suspect it won't come as a surprise to you that as Bob and I have not been getting along very well over the past year, we have now decided to call it a day'.

Now while you may want to be considerate to your family, it is you and your state of mind that is important here. Please don't be afraid to *say* 'If you don't mind I'd rather not talk about all the ins and outs at the moment. It's still all a bit raw and I need to keep it together for the children/work/the dog. I promise to give you all the gory details later, right now I just want to thank you for your support.'

Telling the children

As you can see, I have saved the most important conversation for the last. There is nothing more important in the world than how you tell the children. You may bear the burden of losing your dreams but your children had no choice in the matter. Ending the relationship might have been your choice; it might lead to a better life, one in which you are happier. You have made an educated decision and your children will have to deal with it. If the children are pre-teen, they will have little frame of reference for this sort of experience. They will probably have other children in their class whose parents are separated but, when it happens to them, it will almost certainly be the biggest thing in their life to date.

Breaking it gently

Whatever differences you and your partner may have, you need to pull together on this one. You may no longer be a couple but you will always be parents. Sit down together and decide what you are going to tell the children beforehand. 'We have something important to tell you. You've probably noticed that Dad and I haven't been getting on for awhile and we think it's better that we no longer live together. This doesn't affect our feelings for you, we still love you, it's just that our feelings for each other have changed'. *It is also crucial that your children understand that this is in no way their fault!* 'We want you to know that this decision has nothing to do with how you kids behave. I know we occasionally squabble with you, but we couldn't possibly wish for a more wonderful group of children. This is **totally** about issues between Dad and I, do you understand?' *(Also see the Pocket Primer on page 107.)*

Giving your children a secure future

Parents separating no longer guarantees a life of ruin for a child. Thank heavens we've moved on a bit – BUT it does have to be handled very carefully. First you need to keep in mind that, subconsciously, children consider themselves to be a combination of both their parents. What this means is that when you speak badly about your ex, the part of your child that corresponds with that parent will feel badly. And if, when your child is with your ex, that parent speaks badly about you then the other half of the child will respond emotionally to that. In other words, they will take it personally. If you put together two sad halves then you will end up with one sad whole and I'm sure you don't want that.

Why bad-mouthing your ex can destroy your children

Most of the time parents will swear up and down 'I never *ever* say anything bad to the children about their mother/father. Oh no, I would never do that!' Then you speak to the children and find out that while they may not direct the comments to the children, they will have conversations with all and sundry when the children are in earshot and the effect is the same.

I have had more children tell me 'Mummy always talks about Dad on the phone to Grandma and what she says really upsets me...' than I've had hot dinners. And, of course, as you think the children can't hear the conversations, that's when the inappropriate-for-a-child's-ears information comes tumbling out. So if you don't want to answer questions like 'How come you're going to slap Daddy's secretary' or 'How come Daddy punched Uncle Steve in the eye' keep your conversations for when there is absolutely no chance of being overheard.

What children care about most

The other important thing that will help your child feel as secure as possible is attention to practicalities. Children are basic creatures. They are not uncaring but, quite possibly, no matter what their age, they have not yet developed a level of emotional intelligence to enable them to absorb the ramifications of what is happening. Children, however, do understand their needs and their first worries will often be based around what they know and understand. 'Will we have to move?' 'Do I have to go to a different school?' 'Where will Dad live?' 'When will I see Dad?' 'Will we still go to Nantucket in July?' 'Will Dad still take me to soccer?' 'Will we still get to see Granny and Grandad?' It might seem that, at the time, they don't care or understand – they do care and they understand as much as they can. What they are doing is instinctively checking what in their world is still 'safe'. That is why it is important that you gather all this information together before you have the big conversation.

Simple phrases to help keep them in balance

Go straight from the phrases in the section above into the 'Now don't worry you won't have to move, you'll stay at your school. Your Dad is going to be living ten minutes away and you'll see him…………etc. etc.'

How to move on from this difficult conversation

End the conversation with 'We know this is a lot for you to take on board, so we thought we could maybe sit down again tomorrow in case you think of anything else you might want to ask. And, of course, if you want to talk before then just let us know'. When we had to have this conversation with our son (he was ten) I also gave him a piece of paper the next day with five telephone numbers on it. They were for his godfather, his godmother, his paternal grandparents, my mother, and a close family friend. I told him that I understood that he might want to talk about it and feel uncomfortable discussing it with either of us so he was to feel free, at any time, to call any of them. Three years later and he did take advantage of two of the numbers. My ex and I decided a year and a half ago to take him to a child psychologist for a bit of a road test. He was being so incredibly calm and well-adjusted that we thought he might be burying his true feelings. The psychologist told me afterwards that he really and truly was completely fine. She said that whatever we had done I should write a book about it, so here we are. ☺ It might still be early days; and, if there had been any other way, I would have wanted my marriage to continue. But sometimes life gives you lemons and you just need to make lemonade.

You are still a family

This is a very tricky one and how it is handled will usually depend on the nature of the break-up and the personalities of the people involved. But let me say again – **it's about the children.** If there are no kids involved, you can wave goodbye to your ex and never ever see them again for as long as you both shall walk this earth. But if there are children, that is a luxury you will not have.

Making the rest of your lives easier

There is nothing that breaks my heart more than people asking my advice on what to do because they are about to get married and the one blot on the landscape is that one or other parent is refusing to come because of the possible attendance of the other parent. I have seen this happen time and time again and often, when you ask how long ago the separation occurred, you will find 'oh they split up when I was eleven'. For heaven's sake don't find yourself in that sort of situation, don't do that to your kids – let it go.

It is going to be torturous in the beginning. For the first year after my marriage ended it was all I could do to be in the same room with him. But I religiously battled on. Ten days after he left it was our son's tenth birthday and we went to the seaside for the day – possibly the worst day of my life and it was on the train on the way back that I quietly removed my wedding ring. Then came the first Christmas and I invited him to the house for Christmas lunch. I spent half the day running back to what used to be the marital bedroom, crying my eyes out, composing myself and coming back out.

How did I survive or why did I do it? Because the light at the end of the tunnel was the hope that by doing it I could, in some small way, give my son something that he had been inadvertently robbed of.

Sharing the duties of parenting

How is it now? Three years down the road, most weeks we might have a meal together, Saturday lunch after music school. We go to school meetings together. The school has both of us listed as primary contacts. Homework duties are shared, as are punishments and big decisions. The result of 'being civilized' is that you have a situation where **your child feels part of a family even though you are not still part of a couple.** You will also find that encouraging this kind of atmosphere will make it easier when either of you introduces a new partner.

Being clear about your status

You must also be certain that you have clearly set out the boundaries to explain that, though you all spend time together, you are NOT getting back together as a couple – you must be very clear about that.

Being civil

This is a bit of a hodgepodge topic, but if I had to boil it down to two sentences they would be **Don't make a show of yourself** and/or **To live well now – *that* is the best revenge.**

Let's address the first one. **Dignity** – it's all about maintaining it at all costs. I know you're angry right now, maybe the red mist has even settled in, but you really don't want to look back on this period of time with shame. How to avoid going down the wrong road? Try to avoid 'drowning your sorrows' – that's usually the fastest road to trouble. If there is someone else involved in the situation, try to avoid ALL contact with that person. Your relationship was with your ex and if there is blame to be apportioned, it should be with the person you were in a relationship with, not some stranger. This means no raving loony messages into anyone's answering machine at 2 am – not your ex's, not the new person's. It also means no telling all your friends 'He was rubbish in bed', 'She's lying, those are not real'; you just look childish. Think 'Rise above it' and 'I won't stoop to his/her level' – write it on your sleeve, post it on your mirror, make it your screensaver – do whatever you have to do, but live it, you'll feel all the better for it.

Alternatives to revenge

Now let's move on to the other self-esteem wrecker: **Revenge** – some say it is a dish best served cold, some say revenge is sweet. I'd say it's a dish best not served at all and is a sour taste indeed. I've been there, been so mad I thought I'd never be able to breathe again until I throttled someone, and, of course, I knew who I wanted that person to be. But don't do it. Yes, release your anger – beat pillows, write letters that you're never going to post. Go to the beach and scream until you're hoarse, but then go home with your head held high and get on with your life. As the saying goes, live your life well – as if you're 'just not bothered' – and one day you really won't be.

CHAPTER SUMMARY
Pocket Primer – Telling the Children

1. Keep it simple.

2. Explain the practicalities.

3. Set up a schedule of when they will see the departing parent.

4. Identify the things that will remain the same in their lives.

5. Leave the door open for continuing the conversation.

The relationship has ended. You had a dream, possibly one that you've had for a very long time, and now it's disappeared, and probably not quietly. For one reason or another your world as you know it has totally altered. No matter how much you may wish it, nothing will ever be the same again. You would have gone into this situation with the best of intentions, you worked as hard as you could in the best of faith but it didn't work. You are not a failure, you are not a victim, sadly it didn't work out but you'll pick yourself up and carry on. You'll learn whatever lessons need to be learned and start walking through the tunnel. You probably can't see the light at the end of it right now, but it's there, so, as the song says, 'pick yourself up and get back in the race…' This is life.

Starting Over

❝ I love my past, I love my present. I'm not ashamed of what I've had, and I'm not sad because I have it no longer… **❞**

Colette

Chapter 6
Starting Over

'Watching you walk out of my life does not make me bitter or cynical about love. But rather makes me realize that if I wanted to be with the wrong person so much, then how beautiful it will be when the right one comes along.' Anon

A lot of people nowadays (even the men) are asking – 'What do I do now?' 'What is the most important thing I need to know to start over?' Try as I might I cannot narrow it down to one invaluable bit of information. There are a few and I am going to share them with you, but let us begin with keeping this one thing in mind – it's never too late. I've seen people fall head over heels in love in their 40s, 50s, 60s even 70s. So let's dust off the seat of our pants, get up slowly and hobble back towards the starting line – yes, *again!* But I promise to make it easier this time.

Picking yourself up off the floor

I don't know about the rest of you, but to me there are few things that feel worse than the end of a relationship. There can be a heck of a lot of pain in the ending of a three month relationship. As for the end of a 13 year marriage; I remember lying on a bed in a darkened room with my eyes closed thinking that maybe if I just held my breath long enough…

Taking the first steps

But you do have to 'just pick yourself up and get back in the race, because that's life…' How you deal with your break-up will largely be determined by your circumstances. If you are on your own, then you can have tubs of ice cream and weepy DVDs. Or maybe you're an 'out on the town with your gal pals' kind of person. But if you have children, your options become severely limited – I'm not sure if that's a good or bad thing. On one hand, it keeps you from putting a wastebasket on your head and running around the garden naked screaming (or it should). And having to put out the fish fingers and beans in the evening will (hopefully) keep you from drowning with a bottle of Jack Daniels every night.

Releasing your emotions without frightening the livestock

However, you do have to be careful that while you don't want to scare the children, you do need to safely release your emotions. I think that a period of weeping, wailing and general gnashing of teeth is a good thing, perhaps even a necessity. But then the day comes when you find yourself noticing a bit of sunshine outside the window, or maybe you find yourself singing. Whatever it is, you can take it as a signal that it is high time you picked yourself up off the floor.

You are not a failure

Some people go into any new relationship with what I call the 'one foot out the door before you've even gone in' attitude. This relationship may or may not work and, if it doesn't, oh well. There are a few things wrong with this kind of attitude, the main one being that if you don't commit to success there is very little chance you will achieve it. And, of course, the old 'you get what you focus on' comes into play again so if you don't think it will work then there's a good chance it won't.

The one thing you must always remember

However, if you're someone who goes into each new relationship with the 'this is forever and ever and ever' attitude, the realization that this isn't so can be devastating. What we want to do here is ensure, as best we can, that the damage is not permanent. There are a couple of Big Concepts that we need to work through to make sure we clear out the mess properly.

One, **you are not a failure.** Your relationship might have broken down. It might have failed. It might even have been down to you, but you are not a failure. Yes I know I am repeating this 'you are not a failure' mantra but repetition is the mother of knowledge.

The role of the dream

What is a dream? A vision, an aspiration; something you are hoping for? An ambition you expect to achieve, or a deeply held desire? However you define it at this particular moment in time, you've lost your dream. Losing a dream is almost like experiencing a death. You are grieving for the loss of the person and the demise of a whole collection of hopes and aspirations.

Ask yourself this

There is a major turning point that you need to reach at the end of a break-up before you can start all over again, and it's all about the dream. Ask yourself *what are you most bothered by* – the fact that this person is no longer in your life OR the fact that you've lost the dream.

The turning point

Please don't answer too quickly, this is a really big thought and it holds the key to your future. The moment that you realize, or begin to feel that it is less the loss of the person and more the loss of the dream is the moment you will begin to move forward. You might know it immediately, or it might take you say… 1 year, 7 months, 2 weeks, 3 days. ☺ But whenever it happens is when you'll know you're going to be ok. In the meantime, there are some things we can do to jumpstart the process.

Changing the dream

The next thing we now need to do is change the dream. One of the most important rules in changing anything about your life is being willing to change the plan. If you're doing something and it isn't working, then change it. And if the new thing doesn't work, then change that as well.

Tweak here, tweak there and you will eventually find the plan that accomplishes what you are striving for.

One aspect was wrong – not the entire concept

It is the same thing with relationships. You had a dream; you and Emma or John were going to spend the rest of your life together and live happily ever after – and it didn't work. You tried to fix it but it just didn't work and the dream collapsed. First we have to understand that it was that particular dream that fell apart. Not the dream of you ever finding happiness within a relationship – just the dream of you finding happiness in that particular relationship.

The secret to moving on successfully

So what do we do now? We change the dream. This doesn't mean immediately find a replacement for Emma or John and trying to slot them into the same dream – it means **change the dream.** Or more accurately *create a space for a different dream that will hopefully become your new reality.* This means putting an end to endlessly bemoaning 'what could have been'. It's not going to happen, it's behind you… next!

Setting your new parameters

The one thing I would suggest doing before moving on, however, is to make yourself a small list. Write down all the things that did not work in your last relationship, try not to make it personal. 'Emma was really messy' isn't helpful. 'I am hoping for a tidy house now' is. In other words, by listing the things that didn't work and changing them into positive statements for the future, you are fine tuning your new dream.

Are you really ready?

I could tell you to put a post-it note up on your mirror with the words 'If at first you don't succeed try, try again' on it but trying again is what most of us do anyway. We suffer our first 'heartbreak' in our teen years and, once we learn the lesson that you won't really die from it, we soldier on. Next Prince Charming or Perfect Girl comes around the corner and we're off at the races. Then we usually stumble again and the entire process repeats itself.

Doing a safety-check

It is really important that when you decide to go back out into the world you really are ready. The mistake that a lot of us make is jumping back in before time. Figuring out whether or not the time is right is a bit tricky. Half of us want to run back out the front door before we're ready; the other half (if left to their own devices) would never go out the front door again. Why is this? And what separates us?

What happens if you go back too soon

The half that wants to run right back out are often of the mind that, if they quickly 'fall in love' again, it will erase the pain of the current bust-up. They will swear on their pet pig's head that it isn't what they're trying to do – but it is. Cries of 'Oh I'm not bothered I'm fine' usually mean 'uh-oh this one needs a bit more time'.

On the other side of the divide reside the people who very much felt *every* single drop of pain, and the idea of putting themselves in a position to possibly feel that awful again; well, they just can't bear the thought of it. How do you know when you're ready? I would say halfway down the road from 'I'm not bothered ' and 'I think I'll just sit here in the dark a bit longer'. You probably won't just wake up one day and decide – 'ok I'm 100% fighting fit now'. And most likely, whenever you decide, there might be a bit of nervous agitation at the thought but that's only normal.

1. Do you still find yourself thinking about the person a dozen or more times a day?

2. Do you still feel uncontrollable anger over the end of your relationship?

3. Or sadness?

4. Are you still to be heard declaiming loudly to anyone within earshot 'You do realize that all men/women are *&!!*+^s don't you?'

5. On a scale of 1–10, how would you rate your general state of mind?

If you answer yes to 2 of the first 4 and your answer to number 5 is under 6.5, then you're still not ready.

But let's skip ahead to some of the other tips so you can get yourself up to at least an 8!

How and why – not to become bitter

When a relationship ends, it is difficult not to feel resentful, embittered, cheated or hard done-by. Some of us will also feel cynical about love and wonder whether or not it ever really does work. The saddest of all are those of us who quickly become resigned to the 'fact' that standing in the shards of a shattered relationship is the only place we will ever be.

It is hard not to be bitter and to find a way to heal your pain, but you must make the effort to stave off the bitterness and eventually time will take care of healing the pain.

Survival of the fittest

The secret to not becoming bitter is to think of yourself as a survivor rather than a victim. Why do you think it is that, decades later, the opening strains of Gloria Gaynor's *I Will Survive* has us all running to the dance floor, arms flailing wildly above our heads? And who amongst us doesn't know all the words? That's because that is what we are all looking for – the strength to live to tell the tale. We don't want to be a casualty of a failed relationship. Nor do we want to spend the rest of our life as walking-wounded; we want to rise like a phoenix from the ashes. We don't want to just survive, we want to triumph; and the first step towards achieving that is to permanently delete certain phrases from our vocabulary.

Victim Statement – *'I can't believe he/she did that to me'*.
Survivor Statement – *'I can't believe that whole thing happened but now I'll move on'*.

I am not saying delete all knowledge of what has happened, but stop thinking and speaking like a victim, then you can change the bad memory into a positive hope and become a survivor.

Shedding the black cloud

Call it your aura, the atmosphere that surrounds you, your vibe, your mood – you can be certain that most people can figure out what kind of mood you're in without asking. It is also pretty much a rule that the more intense your mood, the more 'visible' it is. You walk down the street very happy and you'll find strangers smiling at the sight of you. Sit on the bus dejected and down and, if I'm sitting next to you, I will burst out crying because I can feel your pain. I won't know what is wrong with you but I'll know that, whatever it is, you are really hurting. Here's something I've observed over the years – women tend to think they can hide their mood. They usually can't. Conversely, and most strangely, a man who cannot tell you where his other foot or sock is can spot a woman who is under a black cloud from a mile off. And no they don't have to be very intelligent men, or very sensitive men, or any such thing. However, most often they're single men. I don't know if it is a self-preservation technique but I am constantly amazed at how men can look at a woman walking down the street, turn to each other and say 'needy nutter' without exchanging a word. Then they get married and somehow some of them shed the capability to read their beloved's signals at 100 paces. ☺

Making sure the black cloud is gone

Anyway, the point is, if/when you decide (be you male or female) to re-enter the world of relationships and dating, you need to be sure that your black cloud has blown away. If not, you're pretty much wasting your time. If you want to attract a happy, sane, well-adjusted person, then you're going to need to look like a happy, sane, well-adjusted person as well. The danger about going out under the black cloud is that you will often attract someone who, on a certain level, is in the exact same space as you are. Needless to say, two wounded birds do not make a flying team. I know it's hard to imagine getting out from under it, but it will happen. Don't try to push the cloud away. I promise it will gently flow away – but first you must let go.

Putting your baggage in the back of the shed

'Vengeance is having a videotape planted in your soul that cannot be turned off. It plays the painful scene over and over again inside your mind. And each time it plays, you feel the clap of pain again. Forgiving turns off the videotape of pained memory. Forgiving sets you free.' Lewis B. Smedes.

I don't remember exactly when it was that the term 'baggage' went from being a bit of Samsonite to meaning 'the excess emotional detritus of your past that you insist on carrying around with you'. But now, if someone says 'Oh she's got a lot of baggage' you immediately think, oh dear that's going to be three hours at dinner hearing about what this one or that one did to her. We know *you* are not going to be doing that because by now you've already memorized the How Not To Be A Victim mantras.

But in case they haven't yet sunken in, here's a foolproof analogy. You know those little red wagons that kids drag around behind them with their toys, teddy bear, and the raggedy blanket they wee on and won't let you wash? Well, as adults we have them as well.

Why you must dump your baggage

If you ask the average woman who was the first man who broke her heart, she will tell you his name was Calvin Claptrap, he was 9, he had a dog named Boo and he used to wear a striped jumper every Tuesday. She will then be able to list every single man who did her wrong and produce detailed records of the circumstances. And if she digs around under the teddy bear and the raggedy wee'd on blanket, she might even find a teaspoon full of pain as well. After awhile of doing this, the first red wagon gets full so she'll tie a second one on. Soon that one is full so she'll add a third and a fourth. Before you know it, she is having trouble walking up the hill of life because she's dragging this unwieldy cavalcade behind her. Ask the average man the name of the first woman who broke his heart and he'll remember her name, he was usually about 19 and then, after that, he has nothing in his red wagon until you. I've met men who have to stop and think to remember the names of ex-wives! I could go into all sorts of anthropological reasons for why we're all the way that we are, but that's not too much use right here and now so I won't. But what I will do is tell you that in life – ALL areas of life – **success goes to the light of baggage.**

Sorting what little to keep

If it isn't that important – fling it over the side (it's biodegradable). If it is that important, then pick off all the meat, pack the bones in a box; and put the lot in the back of the attic behind the Christmas decorations and the old baby clothes. You don't need it and you'll move faster without it.

A shiny and new external you

One of the things that really gets my goat is this idea that your-life-is-falling-apart-but-here's-a-new-shade-of-lipstick-that-will-make-it-all-ok culture that we now live in. It drives me crazy, and it makes me sad. If you put frosting on a cowpat, it is still going to smell like a cowpat, taste like a cowpat and be a cowpat. If you are down, depressed, angry and whatever other emotions you are struggling under the weight of, a new frock and some highlights are not going to make it all ok.

Treat yourself but don't go overboard

HOWEVER… having said all that, it can help, and no I am not contradicting myself. What I am against is the thought that putting up lovely new wallpaper will miraculously repair the gaping cracks underneath. I have seen too many people do that and pay the price. Men buying big fancy cars, women buying Jimmy Choos. Come the end of the day, you'll either be riding around in a big car still mad and on your own; or tottering along in a pair of stilettos still sad and on your own. A little bit of sprucing up will certainly lift your mood, so feel free to indulge. Just make sure you realize that it might just be a case of hanging new curtains, there is probably still a bit of repair work to be done to get you fighting fit again.

An almost new and improved you (internal)

The temptation, especially if you feel you're the wronged party, is to demand an explanation from either the other person, or the other person's friends, family, or anyone who knew the both of you. 'What do you think went wrong?' 'Did he say anything to you?' – My attitude is slightly different from most on this subject (no surprise there). I think there is not much good to be gained from that line of thought or questioning.

Don't ask questions you don't really need answers to

'Is there anything you'd like to tell me?' or 'Well I'm sorry it didn't work out for us, why do you think that was?' is, in my opinion, as far as questioning should go. There is a really good chance that you're not going to be told the truth. And, frankly, whatever you're told is not going to change the real problem, which is that you're not going to be together anymore. Also it is quite subjective. 'I don't want to be with you anymore because you're too needy'. Well maybe you are but maybe you're not. So you're then going to walk around for the rest of your life thinking that you'll never have a proper relationship because you're too needy and it may not even be so. You would be surprised/horrified at some of the 'excuses' people will throw at you when backed into a corner. I once knew a man who broke off an engagement 'because she never had mayonnaise in the fridge!' I kid you not, that is what he said and she dragged that around in her little red wagon for years after.

" If you were going to die soon and had only one phone call you could make, who would you call and what would you say? And why are you waiting? **"**

Stephen Levine

Learn how to be your own mirror

There is a phrase bandied about a lot these days, it is called being 'self-aware'. Basically, it translates as being aware of what is going on with you to an extent that you know yourself, thereby removing the need for you to be constantly searching for your reflection in mirrors held up by the outside world.

When you ask someone with whom you've just ended a relationship what was wrong with you, and why they don't want to be with you any more, chances are you're holding yourself up in front a dirty, cracked, broken mirror and what you're going to have reflected back at you isn't going to let you know what you really look like.

Understanding what happened

One of the best things you can do for yourself, whenever possible, is to try and understand, for as much as this is possible, exactly what happened. As the saying goes, if you don't understand your history you are destined to repeat it. This is a *very* difficult exercise because it will call for you to take a hard, long look at yourself and right now, frankly, you might not have the strength for that. But if ever there was a good time for a little DIY self-improvement this is it.

Kickstart the healing process

Find something small that you have wanted to work on for awhile, a new exercise regime, learning a new language, taking a philosophy class or taking up Tai Chi. Read a book you've been putting off – anything that will give you a sense of accomplishment. That is what you need to do now, feel good on the inside. Honestly, it does all shine from within and we want to repair any cracks, shed that baggage, ban that dark cloud from over you, all the things we've said so far. So clean the windows of your soul and the light will shine through – sounds a bit hokey but it is oh so true.

What has changed since you last dated

Everything and nothing. The basic principle is still the same. Two people feel a possible attraction and think that spending some time together might be an enjoyable thing. The attraction might be purely physical, it might be intellectual, spiritual, shared morals or political beliefs, or you made each other laugh on Facebook. Whatever it is, the bottom line is you want to get to know this person better in some way and the best way to accomplish this is by spending more time together.

What's new if you haven't dated in five years

So what has changed? Well it depends on how long it's been. **If it's under five years** then probably nothing. Between five and ten years, the ways of meeting people have really expanded. You will notice that many of the people you know (whatever your age or background) will be dating people they met on the internet. They will either have met them on a dating site or some sort of discussion forum discussing anything from politics to who is better, Wu-Tang Clan or Radiohead (bands for the merrily uncool among us). You may also know people who have met on social networking sites, like Facebook. (*If you go back to the second chapter on dating you will see some of the more popular methods we are now using to meet people.)

What's new if you haven't dated in ten years

If it has been **over ten years,** you may find it surprising how much more competition there is. There seem to be fewer men and more women out on the circuit. There are possibly more openly gay men now and, as most women are getting into committed relationships at a much later date, the numbers are a bit unbalanced.

If it is over ten years since you last dated, you may also be surprised at the number of women who now think absolutely nothing of asking a man out on a date. It has become de rigueur – if you've never done it, it might take some getting used to. 'I was wondering if you'd maybe like to go out for

" Whenever I date a guy, I think, is this the man I want my children to spend their weekends with? **"**

Rita Rudner

a cup of coffee sometime' is easy and perfectly acceptable, especially for a newbie. If you find that quite difficult, the old 'A group of us are going to (?) do you fancy coming along?' is really easy. It doesn't feel like you're asking them on a date and you will be less afraid of rejection.

What's new if you haven't dated in over fifteen years

If it's been **15 years or more,** it might take a while for you to get used to one or two things that may or may not have been this way when you were last dating. The distance between saying hello and 'do you have condoms in your handbag?' might be appreciably shorter than you're used to. Do what makes you feel comfortable – if it makes you feel uncomfortable or pressured then don't. And, nowadays, women carry their own condoms – yes I know that does take a bit of getting used to as well. Bad enough we have to stroll through Duane Reade with a carton of tampons we now have to slap down a multipack of condoms at the checkout.

You may also notice a lot more social mobility, less attention being paid to class. You may also notice more intra-religious dating than might have been around before. When you were last out, a Protestant girl and a Catholic boy might have raised an eyebrow but now you wouldn't be surprised to see the Reverend's daughter with a Buddhist or a Muslim. And, of course, the Baptist girl who is dating the ex-Hari Krishna.

What's new if electricity has been invented since the last time you dated

Last, but definitely not least, especially to those of us who have been off the scene for way over a decade, feel free to date whatever age you want to. Many of the women I know who are in their late 40s are dating men who are in their early to mid-30s. No money is changing hands, and there is nothing untoward about it. As we get younger at heart, fitter, happier, more independent, the range of people we attract broadens. Many of the men I know in the younger age ranges prefer older women, finding them more relaxed and comfortable in their skin. So, if someone younger asks you out, throw caution to the wind – you don't need it any more. Needless to say you don't have to run out and find yourself someone to break every social barrier you may ever have been conditioned into – just know that you're pretty much responsible to yourself now, so do as you wish. However, the cardinal rule is still the same 'choose wisely and carefully'…

What has not changed

Everyone wants to have a good time on a date. No one wants to be stressed out and pressured. Everyone wants to feel attractive and interesting. No one wants to be made to feel boring or not worth the effort. No one wants to feel you're only out with them because they will spend a lot of money on you. Neither does anyone want to feel they're being used for one thing or another. And, of course, most of us don't want to feel that sex is the only reason you're there. However, a decade or so ago we would have been able to split this list neatly down the middle based on gender but no more. You're just as likely to find a man complaining 'she only wanted to sleep with me' and a woman saying 'I was so stressed out from work, I just wanted to go home and go to sleep'. Yes there is still *Vive la difference* but now the difference will depend on the individual's personality rather than their gender, and that has made the whole enterprise much more fun.

Regaining confidence in the bedroom

Women: For many of us, this is the toughest hurdle of all. I've had women sitting across from me with tears streaming down their face at the very thought of taking off their clothes in front of someone new. They've been disrobing in front of only one person for a whole lot of years without thinking about it, now it's back to Square One.

Taking advantage of the tricks of the trade

Here's the good news. There is now an entire industry based around showing women how to make the best of whatever they've got. There are about 45 different types of undergarments guaranteed to cure whatever evil befalls you. There are creams, potions and lotions to make sure you have the skin of a new born yak. You can revitalize your hair, whiten your teeth, you name it and you can do it. But you know what is the most important thing of all? – It's self belief.

Belief is the key to success

For anyone else to think you are attractive and sexy, you've got to believe it yourself, *and really believe it*. I know you've probably heard this before, but I am here to tell it to you again because it is the only truth. I've seen women tarted up to the nines who don't believe in themselves and they could be invisible for the amount of attention they're getting. And then I've seen women not nearly as attractive in the conventional sense, but they feel good about themselves and people respond to that.

For many of us, by the time we're out there on the market a second or third time, we're not 'selling' our possible capabilities as baby makers. It's about who we are, the lessons we've learned, the patina of experience that glows off us – that's what makes us attractive and sexy.

Taking charge of who you are

Go take up Tai Chi, take some belly dancing lessons, check out Julie Peasgood's *The Greatest Guide to Sex* – get your mojo working again and it will all be alright on the night. Don't worry about **The First Time.** I have yet to hear of a man who, upon a woman removing most of her clothing, said 'eww' and ran out the door. One of the lovely things about most men is that, by the time they've got their shoes and socks off, wild horses couldn't turn them back. ☺

Men: Jumping into bed with someone other than the warm pair of feet you've been used to for over a decade can be just as scary for men as women. Just as many men worry about their attractiveness and, even more scary, whether or not they will be able to perform. If I had 50 cents for every man who has cried into his soup about losing his hair (gentlemen –

that bothers you, it does not bother us) I would be in the South of France writing this book. And gentlemen, worrying about the fact that you are no longer capable of maintaining an erection for six hours or 'doing it' four times a night – well, frankly, most women I know don't care. Now, if you're going to insist on going out with girls, then I guess you might need to go see a doctor and get some assistance. But if you're going for 'the more mature woman' we don't want you to do it several times a night – just make sure the one time you do it, you do it right. ☺

Doing it all over again

This is a different kind of 'doing it' than we discussed above. This is about the whole thing.

This is about taking the chance at love, companionship, whatever it is that you are looking for. Look, if you get sick eating a bad meal in a restaurant, you may choose not to go back to that restaurant but you certainly don't take a decision never to eat out again. I know that might sound like an overly simplistic analogy but, as my father used to say – keep it simple.

'Yes, but what if I get hurt again?' – Fine, then you reread this book.

It's never too late

I recently met a couple in their 70s who came to me for a kind of check-up on their relationship. They met and married in their late 60s and both of them believe that, for the first time in their life, they are truly in love. They feel that every wrong turn gave them a lesson that they now can use to be committed, dedicated and strong in their relationship with each other. I watched them walk away from our meeting holding hands (having told them that, in my humble opinion, they were more than fine) and when she leaned over and rested her head on his shoulder, I thought 'oh I'd like some of that'. Then when he reached over and patted her backside lovingly I thought 'YES!!!'

CHAPTER SUMMARY
Pocket Primer – Getting Back On The Bike

1. You are never too tired/old/past-it to start over.

2. Your relationship might not have worked out, but that just means it wasn't as right as you originally may have thought. Now you're free to find the right one or allow it to find you.

3. Look at yourself and decide what your good points are. Focus on them and be proud of them. Do it quietly and you will find your self-confidence growing slowly but steadily.

4. Learn to be pleased and happy by yourself, within yourself, and others will naturally gravitate towards you.

5. Yes, you don't have to be with someone, but it is nice…

Compatibility Quiz

66 Age does not protect you from love. But love, to some extent, protects you from age. **99**

Jeanne Moreau

Chapter 7
Compatibility Quiz

A Compatibility Questionnaire

I first came up with the idea for this exercise a couple of years ago, when a television program wanted me to counsel two celebrities who were about to get married. The program wanted to see if there was a foolproof way to determine whether or not two people were perfectly matched. Well, of course, there isn't a guaranteed, impossible-to-fail way. If there was, then there would be no divorce or separation and a lot less unhappiness around.

However, what we can do is identify some possible areas that could cause us trouble down the road, and do a little 'preventative maintenance'. So think of this as surveying a piece of property that you are about to move into. You're probably going to buy it no matter what – you just need to know the how/what/where of repairs.

Please answer the questions separately on individual pieces of paper. And under no circumstance peek at the answers! When you're both finished, go through them together.

Enjoy!

The Questions

Dear Couples

Hopefully, you will find that this simple exercise will be as helpful to you as it has to the many people I've worked through it with. Take it as a template to make your relationship stronger and remember, no one else can tell you whether you're right for each other or not – only your hearts can tell.

All the best

Jenni x

Section 1
Day-to-Day

This section covers the nuts and bolts of your daily existence. Who likes to sleep with the window open, who never tidies up, who leaves the top off the toothpaste and the towels on the floor? Seemingly innocuous when you're deep in the throes of new love, but often the first area where the cracks will start to show.

1. How do you find living with _____ ?

2. What is his/her most annoying personal habit?

3. Have you told him/her about it and what did he/she say/do?

4. What is the best thing about living with _____ ?

Section 2
Making the Commitment

This is about what made you decide to take the next step. Did you want to have a nice party; did someone need immigration papers, were the mammies looking for grandchildren? Important to be clear from the beginning as to 'why now', so that down the road you're not faced with 'well I never really wanted to do it and you made me'.

5. What made you finally decide to take the relationship to another level? You'd been perfectly happy where you were – what made you decide to do this? Did you feel pressurized in any way?

6. What would have happened if both of you were not in agreement about moving forward; would that have caused the end of the relationship?

Section 3
Who is this Person Anyway?

This is about your perception of this person in relationship to the outside world, and your perception of them in relationship to you. 'Everyone thinks he's a thug because he's always punching people in the pub but I see a totally different side to him...'

7. What do you think are the best and worst qualities about
    _____ in relationship to the rest of the world?
    ['She is always there for her family' but 'She never lets anyone get a word in edgeways'.]

8. What do you think are the best and worst qualities about
    _____ in relationship to you?
    ['He is always there for me' but 'He shouts when he gets angry'.]

Section 4
The Moral Maze

Relationships quite often fall down because people have very different moral values. This can become an enormous issue, especially when children enter the equation.

9. Your partner is walking down the street and sees an envelope full of money on the footpath, what would he/she do with it? Take it to the police/buy himself that _____ he's been after/spend it on gifts for you/other choice.

10. You're walking down the street and you see a group of kids harassing a pensioner, what would you do? What would your partner do?

11. There's an election coming up shortly, how important would that be to you? How important is that to _____ ?

Section 5
To Talk or Not To Talk

This is the biggie. Communication. How you regard communication and problem-solving; and how do you do it?

12. What are some of the things you argue about on a regular basis?

13. How do you argue? Sulking/shouting, etc.

14. Who usually says sorry first?

15. How do you make up?

16. When the argument is over does _____ move on or does he/she tend to hold on to it and bring it up again and again?

17. Who starts the most rows?

18. Who usually backs down first?

Section 6
The Hard Times

What do you do when the proverbial hits the fan? Do you work through it or do you ditch and move on?

19. What has been the biggest obstacle your relationship has had to overcome? How did you handle it?

20. Was there ever a time when you thought – right, this is it, and it's over?

21. What made you come back?

22. What is the one thing that _____ could do that would make you walk away?

Section 7
How Deep is Your Love?

What makes you willing to do the work that needs to be done?

23. If your relationship was to end tomorrow, what would you miss the most about _____ ?

24. Close your eyes and try to imagine the rest of your life without _____ in it – how does that make you feel?

The
Answers

Please remember that there is no such thing as a right answer or a wrong answer. These are just guidelines to open up a conversation between the two of you, so you can see if you can identify areas that might need a bit of work before they turn into fully-fledged problems.

You will notice that a few questions don't have accompanying answers. That is because those particular questions are just there to provide more background for that particular topic.

GOOD LUCK!

Section 1
Day-to-Day

This section covers the nuts and bolts of your daily existence. Who likes to sleep with the window open, who never tidies up, who leaves the top off the toothpaste and the towels on the floor? Seemingly innocuous when you're deep in the throes of new love, but often the first area where the cracks will start to show.

1. How do you find living with _____ ?

Often we take for granted how much we enjoy being with our partner. Reminding ourselves, and them, every now and then adds a bit of sparkle to the relationship.

2. What is his/her most annoying personal habit?

Quite often, especially in the beginning of a relationship, people are cautious about expressing a dislike of anything at all about their new lover. That is understandable. However, so is the complete surprise often shown by someone who had absolutely no idea that nothing puts you over the edge more than them going to sleep every night with the television blaring. And if he hasn't told you that the sound of you filing your fingernails makes him want to hide under the bed then you can end up in an enormous row, which could have been easily avoided by a simple conversation.

In tackling this, it is important that you make the statement as mild and gentle as possible. 'I know you are used to being on your own and the television helps you fall asleep, however, it has the totally opposite effect on me; do you think there is a compromise we can come up with?' As in any kind of situation, it is helpful to come to the table with a possible solution.

'I have been checking out cordless headphones as a possibility, how would you like an early Christmas present?' A lot of this stuff sounds totally unimportant but you wouldn't believe how many times couples end up in front of me, and when we start trying to get to the source of what ails their relationship, it stems from a collection of what I call 'simple annoyances'.

3.   Have you told him/her about it and what did he/she say/do?

How people handle these simple conversations will sometimes tell you a lot about possible future 'issues' in your relationship. Someone says 'I'm so, so sorry I had no idea. Yes, let's see what we can do about it'. Or 'You know you're right; I don't like listening to anyone else filing their nails either. No probs, I'll do it in another room or when you're not home'. Then you're on to a winner. However, sulking, 'You're always nagging away at me', or focusing on the telly while you're talking might indicate you need to consider your position.

If you can't discuss simple things without it becoming a big issue then chances are you might find dealing with the big stuff just not workable or not worth it. This is a dangerous place to be because you then fall into the 'it's just not worth the hassle' syndrome. Not good. There is a thin line between calming down and letting everything roll off your back for the sake of peace and quiet – and letting every single thing in the world annoy you if it isn't done in the way you would like it to be done.

4.   What is the best thing about living with _____ ?

What you are looking for here is how quickly an answer springs to mind, and what type of answer it is. Is it 'Oh everything is wonderful but I guess waking up to her smiling face is the best'; or is it 'errrrrm let me think… (10 minutes later) …well I guess, hmmm, I don't know really'. This sort of answer is not a wrong/right answer (none of these are). It just means that you might need to spend a bit more time appreciating and being grateful for your other half's presence in your life.

Section 2
Making the Commitment

This is about what made you decide to take the next step. Did you want to have a nice party; did someone need immigration papers, were the mammies looking for grandchildren? Important to be clear from the beginning as to 'why now', so that down the road you're not faced with 'well I never really wanted to do it and you made me'.

5. What made you finally decide to take the relationship to another level? You'd been perfectly happy where you were – what made you decide to do this? Did you feel pressurized in any way?

It is really important to think this through and be clear about this, if possible. Right now it might not seem important but later in the relationship, at the first sign of trouble you don't want to hear 'Well I never wanted to do it anyway and you made me'. And while one of you might be more keen than the other – that's fine. One of you manipulating the other into moving in or getting married is very much not fine!

6. What would have happened if both of you were not in agreement about moving forward; would that have caused the end of the relationship?

Very tricky because you never want to look as if you are holding someone to ransom to get your own way. However, it is also important that you are honest about what you need to happen to feel comfortable. There are too many relationships where one party really doesn't want to commit but goes along with new arrangements just to keep the peace. Or the other common situation where one person feels the need for a commitment but stays in the relationship against their will, even though the other person won't commit. Either situation will end up with you in a precarious position over time.

Section 3
Who is this Person Anyway?

This is about your perception of this person in relationship to the outside world, and your perception of them in relationship to you. 'Everyone thinks he's a thug because he's always punching people in the pub but I see a totally different side to him…'

7.   What do you think are the best and worst qualities about _____ in relationship to the rest of the world?
     Name three of each: e.g. 'She is always there for her family' but 'She never lets anyone get a word in edgeways'.

Much of the time, our partner shows the outside world a very different person from the one they show us. If you are someone who puts a lot of value in what other people think, this question might be hugely important to you.

8.   What do you think are the best and worst qualities about _____ in relationship to you?
     Name three of each: e.g. 'He is always there for me' but 'He shouts when he gets angry'.

It is really important that you have a solid perception as to the character of the person you are with. You need to know who they really are. It might not seem particularly important now, when everything is ok, but if the relationship hits a rocky patch it will be very helpful in aiding you to understand behavior, which to you might be inexcusable or unexplainable.

Section 4
The Moral Maze

Relationships quite often fall down because people have very different moral values. This can become an enormous issue, especially when children enter the equation.

9. Your partner is walking down the street and sees an envelope full of money on the footpath, what would he/she do with it? Take it to the police/buy himself that _____ he's been after/spend it on gifts for you/other choice.

A recent survey on morals found that our attitude towards what is acceptable and what isn't has changed radically over the years. For some, this isn't an issue, for others it is.

10. You're walking down the street and you see a group of kids harassing a pensioner, what would you do? What would your partner do?

How you regard your role in society might be of great importance to you and, if it is, the answer you get to this might carry a serious amount of weight.

11. There's an election coming up shortly, how important would that be to you? How important is that to _____ ?

Politics and social responsibility can also be a talking point. For example, it would be very difficult for me to be with someone who had little or no interest in such matters, while it might not matter to you at all.

Section 5
To Talk or Not To Talk

This is the biggie. Communication. How you regard communication and problem-solving; and how do you do it?

12. What are some of the things you argue about on a regular basis?

This will help you see if there are certain areas of your relationship that need to be sorted out once and for all.

13. How do you argue? Sulking/shouting, etc.

The way in which you argue is crucial in a serious relationship and has a lot to do with whether or not the relationship will have longevity. *(See pages 52–53 on arguing effectively.)*

14. Who usually says sorry first?

While it is important to apologize when it's necessary, it is even more important that a) you really are sorry and not just paying lip service, and b) that you don't develop a pattern where one person always says sorry just to keep the peace.

15. How do you make up?

Not always s-e-x. Not always expensive gifts. Neither will work over the long run. Important to have a situation where simple and honest dialog is more than enough to clear up a bad situation.

16. When the argument is over does _____ move on or does he/she tend to hold on to it and bring it up again and again?

If after an argument is over, then one or the other of you repeatedly brings it up again then it probably was not properly cleared up. Go back and sit down at the table again.

17. Who starts the most rows?

Is one of you always looking for a scrap? Maybe it's possible that your communication techniques need some work, if you are having more 'scraps' than conversations.

18. Who usually backs down first?

Sometimes it is wise to concede the point but be sure that, however the situation has been resolved, you both feel that you have expressed yourself equally and have been heard.

Section 6
The Hard Times

What do you do when the proverbial hits the fan? Do you work through it or do you ditch and move on?

19. What has been the biggest obstacle your relationship has had to overcome? How did you handle it?

This is helpful to keep in the back of your mind, so that when you come up against other obstacles, you can either use methods that have proven successful in the past or avoid methods that didn't.

20. Was there ever a time when you thought – right, this is it, and it's over?

I don't want you to dwell on this. It just helps sometimes, when things feel difficult to say to yourself 'Well we got over… so this is a piece of cake'. In any serious relationship there are going to be tough times. The longer the relationship, the more you will encounter. Learning to work through them together is one of the most useful tools any couple will ever have.

21. What made you come back?

It is really important that you have a solid perception as to the character of the person you are with, and what your relationship is really all about. It might not seem particularly important now, when everything is ok, but if the relationship hits a rocky patch it is always helpful to be able to remind yourself what it is that you want to hold on to.

22. **What is the one thing that _____ could do that would make you walk away?**

If there is something that you feel would be a dealbreaker, it is important to let it be known at the beginning of the relationship. Not in a confrontational 'If you ever do this I will kill you!' kind of way. But in a quiet 'I think I need to explain that I have very strong feelings about x-y-z and if it happened, it could have serious consequences to our relationship. Is there anything you feel that strongly about as well?

How Deep is Your Love?

What makes you willing to do the work that needs to be done?

23. **If your relationship was to end tomorrow, what would you miss the most about _____ ?**

This is more of appreciating and being grateful for what we have, something most of us just don't do enough of.

24. **Close your eyes and try to imagine the rest of your life without _____ in it – how does that make you feel?**

Don't do this too often, as the feeling can be quite overwhelming. Sometimes, when I do it, I just burst out bawling. But even if you're not over-the-top emotional like me, thinking about life without your loved one will usually give you the energy that you need to keep moving forward.

" Piglet sidled up to Pooh from behind. "Pooh!" he whispered. "Yes, Piglet?" "Nothing," said Piglet, taking Pooh's paw. "I just wanted to be sure of you." "

A.A. Milne

Picture Credits

Cover & Title page © Kurhan/Dreamstime

Page 4 © Kurhan/Dreamstime

Page 8 © Kurhan/Dreamstime

Page 13 © Monkey Business Images/Dreamstime

Page 22 © Özgür Donmaz/iStockphoto

Page 37 © Arrow Studio/Fotolia

Page 40 © MAXFX/Fotolia

Page 42 © Kurhan/Dreamstime

Page 63 © digitalskillet/iStockphoto

Page 68 © Yuri Arcurs/Dreamstime

Page 88 © Drx/Dreamstime

Page 92 © Kurhan/Fotolia

Page 99 © Gina Sanders/Fotolia

Page 108 © hannamonika/Fotolia

Page 125 © Anita P Peppers/Fotolia

Page 130 © Monkey Business/Fotolia

Page 132 © Sharon Dominick/iStockphoto

Page 157 © Monkey Business/Fotolia

Backgrounds (pages 41, 64–66, 87, 107, 131) © Hanhanpeggy/Dreamstime

Backgrounds (pages 145–154) © Andres Rodriguez/Dreamstime

Every effort has been made to credit all copyright holders of the photographs used in this book, however, if there are omissions, the publisher will rectify them in any future reprints/editions.

Index